Working for a doctorate

Children with Emotional and Behavioural Difficulties (1990) and
Stress in Psychotherapists (1996).

Working for a doctorate

A guide for the humanities and social sciences

Edited by Norman Graves
and Ved Varma

London and New York

First published 1997
by Routledge
11 New Fetter Lane, London EC4P 4EE

Simultaneously published in the USA and Canada
by Routledge
29 West 35th Street, New York, NY 10001

© 1997 Selection and editorial matter, Norman Graves and
Ved Varma; individual chapters © the contributors

Typeset in Times by
Ponting–Green Publishing Services, Chesham,
Buckinghamshire
Printed and bound in Great Britain by
Creative Print and Design (Wales), Ebbw Vale

British Library Cataloguing in Publication Data
A catalogue record for this book is available from the
British Library

Library of Congress Cataloging in Publication Data
A catalog record for this book has been requested

ISBN 0–415–14730–1 (hbk)
ISBN 0–415–14731–X (pbk)

Contents

Figures and boxes

FIGURES

BOXES

Contributors

Helen Connell is a freelance educationist and former member of the Pacific Circle Consortium.

Robert Cowen is Senior Lecturer in Comparative Education at the Institute of Education, University of London.

H. W. Dickinson is Senior Lecturer in the Department of Strategic Studies and International Affairs at the Royal Naval College, Dartmouth.

Hazel Francis is Professor Emeritus of Educational Psychology and former Pro-Director (Advanced Studies) at the Institute of Education, University of London.

Norman Graves is Professor Emeritus of Geography Education and former Pro-Director (Professional Studies) and Co-ordinator for Research Students at the Institute of Education, University of London.

Jagdish Gundara is Reader in Education and Head of the International Centre for Intercultural Studies at the Institute of Education, University of London.

James Hartley is Professor of Psychology at the University of Keele.

Denis Lawton is Professor of Education and former Director of the Institute of Education, University of London.

Diana Leonard is Reader in Women's Studies and Education at the Institute of Education, University of London.

Derek May is Senior Lecturer in Educational Psychology at the Institute of Education, University of London.

Jane Savage is Lecturer in Education at the Institute of Education, University of London.

Anne Sims is Research Officer for the National Union of Students.

Ved Varma is an Educational Psychologist.

Introduction

Norman Graves

The original idea for writing this book came from Ved Varma, who wrote to a number of us and asked us to collaborate on the project. As the discussion developed between Dr Varma, myself and other colleagues, it became clear that we needed to produce a book that could provide practical help for those beginning doctoral research. At the same time, we felt that certain issues connected with research needed to be aired since they impinged upon students' performance and could inform students on factors influencing these kinds of studies. Thus we decided that we would include topics concerned with intercultural issues, with gender and with the nature of PhD studies in a historical and comparative context. The latter analysis poses the pertinent question as to how far the 'routinization' of the PhD is stifling the creativity of PhD research. It also became clear that it would be sensible to confine ourselves to PhDs in the social sciences and the humanities rather than attempt to cover the whole field of PhD research.

We begin on an optimistic note, with Denis Lawton, an eminently proficient thesis supervisor, indicating how success may be achieved in postgraduate study. In so doing he covers the whole field from 'Why study for a PhD?' to 'The examination process'. Some of the areas he mentions will be taken up in more detail in later chapters in the book. In the second chapter Hazel Francis dissects the research process in all its aspects and stresses the importance of 'developing an argument', for a PhD is essentially the presentation of a thesis. In Chapter 3 Anne Sims, who has been much concerned with student problems, examines the whole issue of how students may finance a doctorate. This is a very important and practical issue for most students, and one which has changed radically in the recent past. If her conclusions are not optimistic for the student, the information contained about sources of funds is helpful. In Chapter 4 Derek May gives useful advice to students on how to manage their time. Given that so many research students are now part-time students, this is a very important topic. He stresses, however, that individual differences are significant and that what applies in one student's case may not apply to another.

One thing merges into another. Many of the topics considered so far are related to the nature of the supervision process. So in Chapter 5, I look at supervision in terms of how far the student may choose his or her supervisor, how a fruitful relationship may develop between student and supervisor, at the formal procedures to be followed, how to deal with communication breakdown, and lastly how to manage the examination process. But before a PhD can be examined, a thesis needs to be written. James Hartley in Chapter 6 deals with this very practical problem in a way which will be very helpful to those students who find this task difficult. We also thought it might encourage students to hear the stories of three PhD students. Two have already completed successfully their doctorates and one was still in the process of completing her studies at the time of writing. They all show, in Chapter 7, to various degrees, the difficulty of undertaking such studies on a part-time basis, the problems (personal and professional) they had to cope with and how they dealt with them.

The last three chapters are devoted to some of the important issues mentioned earlier. Chapter 8 sees Jagdish Gundara, an expert in multicultural education, looking at the problems of those students whose cultural background is not Western European or North American. He also examines in some detail the cultural assumptions made in UK universities who take on overseas students and how far it would be possible to conceive of a truly intercultural curriculum in doctoral studies. In Chapter 9 Diana Leonard, whose research into gender issues is well known, examines the problems faced by women students in general and certain women students in particular, but shows how, other things being equal, there is little difference between the performance of men and women at that level. Lastly Robert Cowen, who has done distinguished work in the field of comparative education, traces the origin of the PhD and its conceptual structure in Germany, its transplantation to the USA and the UK, its 'routinization' in the USA and the influence this process has had on the British PhD in the present context.

We hope this book will not only be useful to present and future PhD students, but that it will prove intellectually stimulating as well.

Chapter 1

How to succeed in postgraduate study

Denis Lawton

INTRODUCTION

Studying for a PhD is likely to be very different from what you have
probably experienced as an undergraduate or even as a student on a
taught masters course. This idea will probably not be entirely
surprising to you because each level of education is different in some
ways from that which preceded it: GCE Advanced level students are
often shocked by the fact that the demands of A level subjects are
different from those at GCSE; university undergraduates are usually
expected to be even more responsible for organizing their own
learning; masters students usually have a dissertation to write with
only limited direct supervision. All of this is good preparation, but
a PhD thesis is so different that some students never really adjust to
what is required.

Writing a thesis should be an enjoyable, creative experience – and
it often is. But there are many pitfalls which this book may be able
to help you to avoid. Failing to complete a thesis is very common –
far more common than it should be. In recent years universities and
other institutes of higher education have made many improvements
to the conditions offered to PhD students but the situation is still far
from satisfactory. Perhaps a first step is for you to decide whether
you really want to do a PhD. If you do then you should make up your
mind that you will complete and not be one of the too large
proportion who never finish what they start. The fact that you are
reading this book perhaps means that you have already made up your
mind. If so there are still a number of questions you should ask
yourself.

I will return to those questions shortly, but first you might want to
know on what basis I am offering advice. I completed my own PhD

nearly thirty years ago, and for the last twenty-five years I have been supervising the work of others who want to do a research degree. To begin with I was not very good at it; now I think I am, and the completion rates support that view. At first I was not sure what was expected of me in the supervisory role and I am sure I made mistakes. After so many years experience, I now have very clear views on what the relation between a supervisor and a research student ought to be, but even so there is often room for misunderstanding. The possible relationships are countless: generalizations are limited, but there are a few important principles which nearly always apply.

One reason for the existence of difficulties and misunderstandings is that supervisors will often try to adopt a friendly, collegial stance, and it may not be easy for a research student to recognize the difference between a suggestion and a requirement. There is a good deal of interesting evidence from the field of industrial management that in many structured, hierarchical situations subordinates may often interpret a statement by their 'line manager' as a suggestion when it was intended as a command. In the much less hierarchical situation of supervisor and research student that kind of ambiguity can be even more common – sometimes with serious results. A supervisor might, for example, say that a questionnaire could be improved by a second draft being piloted before being used in the main sample; the research student in this case will need to clarify whether this is a suggestion or a requirement. The social skills required in the relationship are not all on the side of the supervisor, although an experienced tutor will be careful to try to avoid such ambiguities. Even so the research student will often need to be sure about what is meant during the supervision interview – even at the risk of temporarily changing the relationship. Clarity will be better in the long run. Few supervisors want to be put into a situation where they have to say 'I insist that you . . .'. A sensitive student will learn to avoid the necessity for such commands. For a full treatment of the problems of supervision see Chapter 5.

So the requirements of doing research successfully include not only subject knowledge and research training – many interpersonal skills will be needed too. Most researchers will experience embarrassment or even pain at some time during the course of their PhD. Most will have moments when they wished they had never started. The first suggestion is that you should be very sure that you really want to do a PhD before you go too far.

WHY STUDENTS WANT A PhD

It would be a good idea to start by examining your aspirations, motives and long-term goals. It is usually a mistake to embark on a research degree because you have nothing else in mind. To get a PhD will involve years of hard work and all kinds of difficulties. So why do you want a PhD?

Have you a particular interest in research as a process or activity? Are you so interested in a particular subject that you want to continue working within it? Is there a problem you have identified that you think you could solve (or at least throw some light on)? Or are you interested in a job where a PhD will improve your chances of appointment or promotion? Are there other relevant motives?

The more of the above that you can honestly say 'Yes' to the better. Most people have a mixture of motives for starting anything as serious as a research degree. But even so, affirmative answers may not be enough. If your dominant interest in life is, for example, romanesque architecture, it does not necessarily follow that you should start a PhD on it. You might be better advised to write a book on the subject. I have often given that advice to potential students – sometimes mature students – who want to write a PhD thesis on a subject which they find interesting. A PhD might be a good idea, but there are alternatives – writing a good book or producing a first class catalogue might be better. A PhD thesis may impose too many constraints on a potential writer who may only want to learn more about a topic or to create something interesting. A research thesis has to be written in a certain style, obeying academic conventions about referencing and constructing bibliographies which some find extremely irksome. If so, why do it if you do not have to? It may be a good discipline or it may provide good training for some kinds of research activity. But it may not. It is essential to work out your reasons as well as the alternative options early on.

You should also try to develop a clear notion of what a PhD ought to be. In my experience, there are two kinds of PhD thesis (in the humanities/social sciences/education field). One view is that a PhD must be a piece of scholarly enquiry, deliberately limited in scope, but perfectly executed – a 'masterpiece' in the tradition of craftsmen who demonstrate their competence at the end of an apprenticeship by producing an example of work without any blemishes. The other view of a PhD is that it is a worthwhile learning experience. An external examiner who inclines to that view may well ask, towards the end of the oral examination, 'If you were starting this research all over again, what would you do differently?'

These two views might be better regarded as two extremes of a continuum, and that in reality a PhD will often exhibit characteristics of both models. But some topics may lend themselves more to the second model rather than the first, whilst some supervisors (and external examiners) may have the first model firmly in mind. There are certainly some aspects of a thesis where imperfections should not be tolerated – for example, there is no real excuse for having uncorrected errors in a bibliography, or even having a bibliography which is inconsistently presented. (There are several conventions possible but you have to stick to one of them.) In either case a PhD is seen as a training programme which is designed to demonstrate competence as a researcher within a limited field.

In some respects the Humanities and Social Sciences do not lend themselves to 'perfection'. Nevertheless, it is important to have a good match between topic and supervisor. To achieve a good match the research student must know why she wants to write the thesis. And in addition the research student must have a strong desire to finish the PhD. Many fall by the wayside, and although they will probably have benefited in some ways, failure to complete is nearly always a very negative and frustrating experience.

THE HIGHER EDUCATION INSTITUTION

Once you have decided that you really do want to start a PhD you should think carefully about where you should do it. There is usually a choice, and you should make the best choice possible. You should also be aware of the fact that universities and higher education institutes want research students – especially good students – who will not only complete their degrees but also make a positive contribution to the life and work of the university. There will be a selection process of some kind, but before discussing that, it may be useful to see the whole issue from the point of view of the university or the university department.

Why do universities want PhD students?

Research is an important part of university work. In recent years universities have been encouraged to write 'mission statements', which without exception mention research as one important aspect of their work – often the most important one. Universities also get funded to do research and to have a number of research students – if they do not meet their target numbers they lose income. Research students also pay fees. But some universities are better than others, and some departments are better than others – better both at doing research and looking after research students (and the correlation between the two may not be very high!).

Research students should find out all they can about a department long before applying for a place. Specialist journals such as the *Times Higher* publish annual 'league tables' of research ratings. They are important, but it is even more important to know how well a department trains its research students, and this is only indirectly reflected in the published ratings. Evaluations of research are more concerned with the quantity and quality of research publications than with the quality of research supervision, although in recent years the 'completion rates' for each department have been scrutinized. But a more revealing indication will be to discover how satisfied the research students are with the conditions in their department. They can be asked how satisfied they are with the kind of training they have received, the kind of computer facilities that exist, the accommodation available for research students, the adequacy of the library, and above all, the formal and informal arrangements for monitoring the progress and well-being of the research students. If you are contemplating doing your research degree in a university unfamiliar to you, it is well worthwhile spending a few days on the new campus to make the necessary enquiries. This may seem an extravagance, but it is really a good investment. Do not forget that the PhD will take from two to four years of your life: you are risking a great deal. In comparison with the risk, a few days may be very well spent.

University departments should only take students who they think will do well and complete their theses, but some departments, and some individual supervisors, have poor reputations for making adequate arrangements for their research students. Apart from making formal enquiries, it is worth asking at the Students' Union or, if you know students at the university, ask them. You should also collect the names of university teachers who are available for research supervision in your subject and discretely ask lecturers at your own (first degree) university. Such information can be available at great distances – if you ask the right people. It is by no means uncommon in my institution for Australian students to ask for a specific supervisor.

Some university teachers enjoy teaching research students; others regard them as a waste of valuable research time. It is important to find out who belongs in each category. It is easier to express a preference for a specific tutor at this stage than to ask for a change of supervisor later on. (It is not impossible, and it may be necessary, but if you can avoid the embarrassment by getting the right supervisor from the beginning, so much the better.)

I have occasionally given advice to university teachers that if they do not actually enjoy supervising research students, they should not do it. I am sure this is good advice, but it is often not taken, for a variety of reasons. A university teacher may 'need' a few research students to justify his existence in terms of teaching load (increasingly university teachers have a target teaching load; taking on research students who never complete is a very unsatisfactory short-term solution to the problem of reaching a 'norm', but it does happen).

Another problem may be that the best supervisors of research students may not have any vacancies. Different universities or departments have different conventions, but in most there is a notional maximum or even a compulsory maximum number of research students per teacher. This is sensible because supervising research adequately involves such a close relationship and so much time (if done properly) that most teachers prefer not to have more than about ten research students: above that it is very difficult for teachers, even those with superb memories, to carry enough detail to be an effective research supervisor. (The best supervisors will keep very good records of each student's problems and progress, but even so, there are limits.)

The selection process

You will almost certainly be invited to attend the department for an interview before being accepted as a research student. This is likely to be an interview with the departmental research degrees admissions tutor rather than with a potential supervisor. That will come later. At this preliminary interview the admissions tutor will try to satisfy her/himself (and her/his colleagues in the department) that an applicant has the right kind of academic background, as well as the personality requirements for completing a degree which I described briefly above. At this stage the applicant will be expected to have a reasonably clear idea of a research topic – a proposal, preferably in writing. This need not be a fully worked out outline of research but it should reflect sufficient thought about the question or problem to satisfy the admissions tutor that you are both qualified to undertake the research and capable of seeing it through. If all goes well at this stage, you may be invited to write further details of your proposal and then to discuss it with a research supervisor. It is at this stage, or perhaps even earlier, that you need to make a decision about the supervisor who has been suggested. The better prepared you are at this stage the more likely it is that you will get what you want. Too many prospective research students attend for interview having only the vaguest idea about what they want to do, what research techniques will be involved, and not even being familiar with the existing literature on the subject of their research topic. In order for you to get what you want out of a department, you should be aware of what their priorities are, and – to some extent – prepare yourself for the interviews accordingly. Knowledgable students can turn what is intended to be a selection process into a two-way negotiation.

WHY SOME STUDENTS FAIL

Kinds of 'failure'

First we should define failure in the context of research degrees. Comparatively few students complete their theses and still fail; but a high percentage of students never complete (the figures vary considerably from subject to subject, department to department, supervisor to supervisor – you have been warned!). If a student has a reasonably good supervisor and submits a thesis for examination with the approval and support of the supervisor, that student is statistically very likely to pass.

There are, in most universities, two other possibilities. The examiners may decide that there is some merit in the thesis but that further work is necessary either to repair an omission or possibly to re-write a few chapters. A frequent requirement is for the final chapter to be re-written in order to provide a more comprehensive summary and conclusion. The examiners will specify a time limit to complete this *referral* (this requirement is not a failure – a thesis declared to be a failure means that no repair work will make it good enough). The time allowed for a referral will be within a maximum specified by university regulations – often eighteen months. A final possibility, within the regulations ordained by most universities, is that the examiners can pass the thesis subject to their being satisfied about *minor corrections* to be completed usually within a month (anything taking longer than a month being regarded as needing referral rather than minor corrections). The minor corrections may range from something as simple as a few spelling mistakes (even good students are sometimes surprisingly careless about authors' names), or completing a bibliography, or even re-writing a few pages of the text.

Causes of failure or non-completion

So far I have been discussing 'how' students fail rather than 'why'. That is a more difficult question. I know some very clever individuals who have failed, and others who were originally regarded as less gifted academically who succeeded. Why? One reason is that point I started the chapter with: PhD work is qualitatively different from the kind of studying that probably preceded it. Possessing three A grades at GCE A level and a first class honours degree in the chosen subject are useful predictors of success but are certainly not guarantees of success. Other qualities turn out to be much more important.

Apart from developing desirable work habits and attitudes of mind, to which I shall return, there are certain other prerequisites to successful thesis writing. The first is choosing a suitable topic. I mentioned above that there are two views of the PhD: a perfect small-scale piece of research study, or a worthwhile learning experience. There is a third view which students often begin with and have to be talked out of: it is a topic or a problem so complex and enormous that it would take a lifetime's work to complete. I call that view the *magnum opus* type of PhD, which if persisted with will probably never be completed.

A key word to bear in mind when choosing a research topic is *manageability*. Whilst being sufficiently interesting to keep you going for two or three years (preferably not much more), it must not be so complex that it does not allow for normal PhD treatment and completion in a reasonable time. This rules out, for example, many longitudinal studies which might be very tempting but for the time involved. Although I recommended that you should have a research topic in mind before seeing the departmental admissions tutor or your potential research supervisor, you should also be prepared to negotiate – especially on grounds of manageability where the experience of the supervisor should outweigh your own desires. Probably the advice I have given more frequently than any other to PhD students is 'Do not collect more data than you will have time to analyse!' And that advice should probably be followed by 'Data *always* takes longer to analyse than you think it will – much longer'. In other words, selecting a good manageable topic often means cutting down to size your first grand idea. This may mean sampling, or limiting the range of the research – or perhaps both. For example, in some educational research, it may be advisable to remove one variable by studying only boys or girls but not both. (Some kinds of research may, of course, demand an investigation of gender differences, in which case removing other variables will probably be necessary.)

If your supervisor simply accepts your topic without offering any suggestion for 'pruning' or any other kind of improvement, it may be a good idea to take the initiative yourself by checking the main points of manageability with him or her. For example, by initiating discussion:

Is it a feasible topic?
Is there enough in it for a PhD?
Am I proposing to collect too much data?
What about the methodology?

Developing a good relationship with your supervisor

I have already mentioned how important this is, as well as beginning to discuss a few crucial areas of the relationship. It is difficult to give general advice because no two students are the same and all supervisors operate in different ways. But it is possible for the research student to play a positive role whilst ensuring that the relationship is a good one. The research student should consciously consider from time to time whether the relationship is as good as it should be. If the answer is no then you should consider whether any action on your part could improve it. Do you always keep to agreed schedules? Do you arrive for supervisions on time? Do you avoid pestering your supervisor with trivial questions outside the scheduled supervision times? (If you see your supervisor by chance on campus and s/he asks 'How are you?', s/he is not really expecting a detailed review of all your research problems.)

On the other hand, it may be up to you to establish certain routines.

Some supervisors will take the initiative on a number of crucial points of procedure; if they do not then you must. It is your thesis; the major responsibility for it is yours; you must be quite sure that you are doing the right thing at every stage. It may be a mistake to expect too much to come from your supervisor. For example, if the supervisor says 'Come and see me again whenever you want to/when you are ready', you might counter this by taking out your diary and asking 'Would a fortnight today be convenient? . . . At this time?' By this ploy you will have established a routine; after your second supervision, you could go further and make it, say, every other week at a specified time, unless other arrangements have to be made. (They probably will, but a regular routine to deviate from is better than 'Come and see me whenever you like'.)

If you deviate from the routine make sure it is for a good reason. If you have promised a draft chapter by Wednesday and you have not finished it, let your supervisor have an incomplete draft, accompanied by an explanatory note, saying, for example, 'I got stuck. . . . I know it is not complete and not very good but I thought you should see it as it stands now.'

Developing a good working routine with your supervisor

When you have established a regular time and place (avoiding pubs, restaurants and other non-formal sites), it is important to include other aspects of the routine. A few days before each scheduled supervision you should deliver whatever is to be discussed at the supervision: for example, an outline of the thesis, a provisional list of chapters, a draft chapter, a choice of research methods, etc. This document can be usefully headed 'For discussion at tutorial on . . . date . . . time'. In nearly all cases, having something in writing to discuss has many advantages: it is more specific; it avoids misunderstandings and ambiguities; it is more businesslike – having an agenda avoids the danger of the supervision dissolving into general chat. And today when I say having something in writing, this necessarily means having something neatly typed, not handwritten – you must make the supervisor's task as easy as possible. A supervisor today has a right to expect that all research students should be computer-literate – at least to the extent of being competent at word processing. If you are not, put this right as soon as possible – preferably before submitting anything to your supervisor: first impressions are important. And you must keep an exact copy yourself. (Never, never entrust your only copy to anyone – including your supervisor!)

You now have a supervision time with a document to discuss. The supervisor *should* have read it before the appointment; if s/he has not, be tolerant – perhaps go through it with her/him, summarizing the main points and especially noting any decisions you are asking to be made or specific points of advice you need. Make a point of writing down any such advice given by the supervisor, and before the end of the supervision meeting check that you have got it right by reading it back to him. You thus have an agreed record of the meeting which you should file away systematically. Wise supervisors will themselves keep a note of the meeting – for the record – and send you a copy of his version of reality. This may seem very formal, even bureaucratic, but in my view an agreed record of each meeting is essential, although there may be all sorts of other ways of keeping such records.

A good work pattern has now been established with a sequence understood – even taken for granted – by both supervisor and research student:

Supervision No. 1: to discuss document delivered beforehand; discussion; record of discussion (noting in particular any decisions made and the agreed task for the next meeting); time agreed for next supervision; delivery of agreed document in time for the supervisor to read it beforehand; Supervision No. 2 . . . and so on for several years!

If this sounds very mechanical, you should not worry. A good routine is an essential aspect of good supervision – even if you deviate from it occasionally. The pattern for vacations will, of course, be different. You must not expect your supervisor to be available during vacations: this is the time when many academics want to concentrate on their own research. Your supervisor may be prepared to see you, but the offer should come from her/him, not be requested by you. Your task is to schedule your work so that the vacation can be used for a longer piece of work not requiring supervision: catching up on reading, for example, or doing some routine data analysis, or completing a difficult piece of writing which can be presented to the supervisor at the beginning of the next term. Having something positive to start a new term with is good for personal relations.

Developing good work habits

The first requirement is to plan your working day. (More will be said
on this in Chapter 4: here I am primarily concerned with your own
attitudes of mind and developing good relations with your supervisor.) You should work out a pattern for a normal working day: are
you an early morning person, or someone who prefers to work late
at night? Plan accordingly – do not drift aimlessly from day to day!
Plan carefully and deviate from the plan only if there are good
academic reasons for doing so.

There is a story told of Somerset Maugham who invited a budding
novelist to stay with him in his villa in the South of France in order
to have sufficient peace and quiet to write his great work of fiction.
One morning Maugham found him sitting in the sun, and asked him
why he was not writing. 'No inspiration today' was the reply.
Somerset Maugham immediately ordered him back to work: '1,000
words a day – every day – with or without inspiration. Then come
out and enjoy the sun.' This was probably good advice for a trainee
novelist; it is certainly excellent advice for a researcher. Never wait
for inspiration: get on with the work of the day of some kind, whether
you feel like it or not. And 1,000 words a day is not a bad target.

If you are a part-time student then time is probably even more
precious and you will find it essential to plan your working week in
some way. Blocks of time need to be set aside – the odd hour is likely
to be more of a frustration than a help. It is not easy, but without
such discipline the thesis will probably never be completed. Your
schedule will need to include a careful balance between reading,
writing, data collection and so on. Every thesis will be different, but
a pattern of some kind is essential. Your supervisor may well be able
to give you helpful advice on this. If not, work out a pattern for
yourself and ask the supervisor if it seems reasonable.

Your supervisor may also advise you on other aspects of your
routine – for example, keeping records. If not, it is important for you
to develop your own good habits, routines and skills. Many research
students reach the final stages of their thesis only to find that a few
essential items are missing from the bibliography. They can then
easily spend days or even weeks of frustrating searching in the
library for what should have been stored automatically in a filing
system of some kind.

The advice I used to give was to set up a simple card box system:
a five inch by three inch (12.5cm × 7.5cm) card for every book or

article you read (or that you note as wanting to read). The card should be set out in one of the standard conventions. I recommend the Harvard convention for simplicity, but any style will do, as long as you are consistent and record all the necessary details: author's name(s), plus initials, date of publication, full title, place of publication and name of publisher in the case of books. The size of the card still leaves room for a few notes – but that is optional. The advantage of such cards is that they are small enough to enable you to keep a few with you at all times – especially when browsing in the library.

I said that was the advice I used to give: it is still an excellent system, but today many prefer to feed the information daily into their computer. Fine! But I am old-fashioned enough and cautious enough to recommend keeping the cards as well and file them away in alphabetical order in a card box. Boxes of cards are less likely to be stolen than computers and computer disks. For example, a few years ago one of my part-time students who had been working on an interesting PhD for three years was burgled. He lost not only his computer but also all his back-up disks. He telephoned me in panic; I assured him that I had copies of all the chapters he had completed and that we could probably salvage his work from that. But his data was all on missing disks and the analysis was incomplete. He decided to abandon the thesis.

That, of course, illustrates the need for another precaution which I urge upon students but know that many ignore. Computer training usually involves encouraging students to back-up everything they do onto spare disks. That should be taken for granted. But my supplementary advice is not to keep the back-up disks in the same place as the computer, preferably not in the same house – in case of fire. And do not keep them in your briefcase either. Once again risk can be avoided by sensible routines.

THE REQUIREMENTS OF A RESEARCH THESIS

I have already said that there are two views of a PhD and that neither view should encourage students to embark upon their *magnum opus*. I have also stressed manageability. On the other hand, the thesis should make some kind of worthwhile contribution to the chosen field of knowledge. One of the advantages of supervising a PhD is that the supervisor adds to her/his knowledge and expertise. It is the ideal teaching situation: the supervisor begins by being the expert who guides a new scholar through unfamiliar territory; but by the end of the thesis the research student will probably be more expert on that specialized topic than the supervisor. The supervisor will have done what all good teachers aim at – making themselves unnecessary by teaching the student to teach himself.

So, a PhD must contain an element of originality, but originality is of many kinds: it may involve the discovery of new facts or a new method of interpretation, or may take many other forms. Research students should not be too worried about the originality – originality is most likely to emerge from hard work. Your supervisor will advise you. One possible approach in the Humanities and Social Sciences is to identify an area where there is an unsolved problem of some kind – for example, why do so many primary school pupils, especially boys, find learning to read so difficult? The next stage might be to undertake a review of the existing literature on the subject, and then to identify any gaps in our research knowledge. If you can find a gap in the literature that might well be the space for your original contribution. Then you try to make the research investigation manageable – cutting it down to size without making the exercise so limited that it becomes meaningless. It is at this stage that the expert advice of a good supervisor is most needed.

There will be data to be collected, analysed and interpreted. How? Once again, your supervisor will advise. Do not charge ahead with a questionnaire or interview schedule or any other research instrument without first getting the approval of your supervisor. There are few things supervisors dislike more than being presented with data that has been badly collected, and asked for advice to put it right – it is probably too late. Such a situation should not arise, and would not if there were regular and frequent discussions between the supervisor and the research student. If your supervisor is away for a few weeks, do not risk going ahead with data collection without permission. It is likely to be false economy of time and is also the surest way of damaging relations with your supervisor.

All this time you will have been building up your bibliography – systematically, consistently and correctly. There are two conventions and you should check with your supervisor which one s/he favours. And it may vary from subject to subject. The first convention is that you should include in the references every book, article or other source that you have referred to in your text – and only those. The second convention is that as well as the above you also include any major texts which have influenced your thinking about your research topic – not the Bible and Shakespeare, not every book that you have ever read, but any text which has had a significant impact on the way that you have thought about the subject or treated the investigation. In either case it is important for the references to be accurate in all respects. At some stage it will be necessary for you to cross check every reference in your text with the items in the list of references at the end of your thesis. The check is partly to make sure that all the necessary items are included, and partly to ensure that the details correspond – including the spelling of authors' names. A useful convention is to distinguish between books and articles in journals. The Harvard convention does this very simply by underlining the titles of books, but not underlining the titles of articles but instead underlining the name of the journal. The journal article should also include full details of the volume number and pages – not underlined.

Some students find all this very tiresome. They think that what really matters is the quality of the writing and the ideas. True, but you will not get a PhD unless you are also prepared to obey the conventions of research writing. If you think that the rules of the club are too much bother, then you should not join!

THE EXAMINERS AND THE EXAMINATION

All UK universities operate within a system of internal and external examiners. This system includes the examination of research degrees, but in a slightly different way, partly because it is an examination for a single individual and because it involves a *viva voce* or oral examination. Formerly, it was possible – in some universities – to have the supervisor as an internal examiner, but that was sensibly changed a few years ago. In most universities now the supervisor may attend the oral examination (if the candidate wants her/him to) but may not play any part in the discussion or the decision making.

The examination for a PhD is normally based on the thesis including a *viva voce*. But there is usually provision for other forms of examining to be included as well, if, for example, it is thought desirable to set a written paper to test adequate background knowledge or for any other reason. The examination will be conducted by one or more internal examiners together with one or more external examiners who are expected to be experts in the field of the thesis. The normal pattern is for there to be one internal and one external who will read the thesis, submit separate reports, and then conduct a *viva* together, followed – if they agree – by a joint report incorporating their recommendation. If the examiners disagree and the differences cannot be resolved, then most universities have arrangements in their statutes for appointing one or more additional examiners.

Universities take the responsibility for appointing examiners very seriously, and aim to have examiners who are specialists in the field. Some universities have lists or panels of subject experts available in other universities. Examiners will read the thesis very carefully, probably more than once; the criteria for passing or reaching the required standard of academic excellence are roughly the same in all UK universities, although the detailed procedures may differ slightly. Examiners, in addition to writing a detailed report, are required to confirm that originality of some kind has been demonstrated and that the thesis has been written according to established standards. Examiners must also say that the thesis is worthy of publication either in its entirety or in parts. Above all, examiners tend to want to be satisfied that the researcher has become an expert in the chosen field and has demonstrated competence to do the kind of research that s/he set out to do.

Examining all this could be achieved simply by reading the thesis, so what is the purpose of the *viva voce* examination? It is sometimes suggested that the purpose of the *viva* is to establish that the candidate is the author of the thesis by answering questions about it. Only rarely is the authenticity of the authorship an issue, however, and that question will only rarely be the main function of the oral examination. Examiners are more likely to want to satisfy themselves that the candidate has a thorough understanding of the topic, including its background literature. They may ask questions about books or journal articles included in the bibliography, as well as well-known texts which have not been mentioned. There is also usually an element of 'defending the thesis' in the *viva*: a candidate may be asked why s/he used certain research methods rather than others, and asked to justify the choice. S/he may also be questioned on the analysis and interpretation of the data.

The candidate is expected to defend his or her research, and it is important that s/he should not simply accept alternative suggestions from the examiners without justifying his or her own methods and conclusions. Part of the purpose of the *viva* is certainly to demonstrate that a candidate has acquired sufficient knowledge to argue against other points of view. On the other hand, a legitimate question may sometimes be 'Is there anything you would now do differently?'

This is a good question, but has to be handled carefully – and honestly. It is important to be able to justify methods used and conclusions reached, but most researchers would admit that given more time or money some improvements might have been made. In addition, with the benefit of hindsight it is sometimes possible to profit from experience by seeing a better way of achieving results – but without invalidating the existing conclusions. The research student must demonstrate that s/he is capable of carrying out a good piece of research, but s/he will be expected to have learned a great deal in the process.

It is difficult to generalize about what might 'come up' in a *viva*. Prediction is difficult, but a sympathetic supervisor can often give good advice on the best way to prepare for a specific *viva*. You should not expect a detailed dress rehearsal, but some helpful coaching is sometimes possible and perfectly legitimate – it is all part of the training and learning experience of the research student.

CONCLUSION

Two final points of advice about working on the thesis. First, research is difficult – more difficult than most other things you have to do in life. It is made more difficult still by the fact that some aspects of the research will require the student to pace her/himself – that is, to work according to a self-imposed schedule. The problem is that there is always something easier to do than the research: a letter to write, a phone call to make and so on. Avoid saying 'I will just do this and then get on with the research.' This is mere procrastination and a formula for getting behind. Get on with the scheduled research first, and leave those other 'urgent' things until later. Research comes first is the only policy likely to succeed.

Second, most research students need more supervision advice than they think they need. When in doubt consult your supervisor, remembering that if you fail or do not complete then this will count as a failure for the supervisor as well.

If you bear all these points in mind then there is no reason why you should not succeed in your postgraduate study; and you may even find it an enjoyable experience.

Chapter 2

The research process

Hazel Francis

It would be a mistake to give the impression that the research process is simple or singular. There are many ways of carrying out research, but this chapter will not set out possible research methods, nor even the epistemologies that lie behind them. Each discipline has its own literature devoted to the nature of knowledge and to research methods to expand it; but for the purpose of this chapter, namely to help doctoral students to understand the nature of the work in order to cope well with it, it makes sense to treat the research process as a single experience for the individual researcher.

Such experience is perhaps best regarded as integral to, rather than separate from, the researcher and his or her life. It changes people, not simply in terms of technical expertise and knowledge in their field, but also in terms of the ways they value themselves and their work. Working for a doctorate is a seriously large chunk of adult life when responsibilities of employment and family may bear heavily and at times be absolutely demanding. A self forged through tackling the difficulties of research, especially when stress from other sources is high, is a new self. So is the self that overcomes the doubts about ability to do the work. If this can be said by students undertaking dissertations for masters degrees as in Hampson's (1994) report, it applies much more to those working for doctorates.

Serious personal challenge is rarely easy – a great deal of work is involved – and most doctoral students find the process one of mixed fortunes and mixed feelings. Whilst some of the 'downs' could be avoided by improved conditions of work and relationships with supervisors (Eggleston and Delamont, 1983) others require action by the student and yet others seem to be inescapable. The 'downs' are often associated with review of the decision to undertake a research degree, and the research process is such that doubts may often arise.

Some occasions for review are embedded in formal institutional procedures, some arise in the course of the work, and yet others follow changes in researchers or in their lives. More will be said on review later in the chapter.

Help to cope with the emotional turmoil, sharing the pleasures and the pains, is as important for researchers as is the tutorial supervision of their work. Friendship helps a great deal – so does the opportunity to bounce ideas and feelings off others also engaged in research. Work with a supervisor is the richer if there is strong shared interest in the work and in each other's ideas about it; and most is gained from the research process by finding a balance between individual drive and autonomy and the engagement and support of others. One of the most satisfying aspects of the process for both supervisor and student is the emergence or strengthening of a competent researcher, personally wiser and more confident in their work, and fit to take their place in the research community.

INITIAL COMMITMENT

As in most things it is important to make a sensible start. It may be useful to think about applying for admission to a programme or course as being like applying for a job (although it entails paying out rather than earning). As well as wondering about being interviewed or accepted there are questions about the job itself. Are circumstances and attitudes such that there is an expectation of staying with it, come what may, or is there preparedness to consider leaving if it really doesn't suit or is not working out? Those who prepare themselves and their friends and families for the possibility of non-completion are spared some of the worst anxieties endured by students when work is difficult or circumstances change. There is no guarantee of the job working out. Unless this is fully understood by all concerned, including university staff, the pressure for successful completion may be self-defeating.

The fact that most students succeed, some against tremendous odds, suggests that in spite of difficulties they find the work appealing. What is it like? The subjective experience of many who have tried it has been of a sort of culture shock – of a switch from earlier work on predominantly taught courses to a course which is supervised rather than taught, and where success is dependent on original and autonomous work.

It pays then to find out as much as possible about the expectations and practices in the department or departments to which application is made. Information may be available at two levels – university regulations for the research degree and departmental practices of working with students. The former are very similar from one university to another and are general in nature. They specify conditions for registration, the minimum period of registration before a thesis can be submitted for examination, the examination requirements concerning length of thesis, oral examination and any other assessment, and the criteria for success. These last are usually that the work be rational, substantial, original, and a contribution to knowledge in the field concerned. In essence they derive from the tradition of doctoral work in Germany, a tradition which spread to the United States before taking root in Britain (Noble, 1994). More about this in Chapter 10.

Departmental regulations and practices are detailed interpretations of the general regulations, honed to fit different academic fields and to specify the conditions for work and support for students. Any department worth its salt will now have a printed document spelling out what is expected and provided. It is a sort of job specification which carries information about the kind of work to be done, usually in terms of product and attendance requirements, and about the 'boss's responsibilities to the worker'. It says what can be expected from supervision, what procedures are adopted for reviewing work, what facilities are provided for research, and how to seek help if in difficulty (including the tricky business of not getting on with a supervisor and what to do to appeal against any decision concerning continuation or assessment, see Chapter 5). Many students see this as part of the paperwork around entry to a course and forget they have it for possible future use. This is a mistake, because it means possible neglect of useful support facilities and possibly a greater sense of uncertainty at work than is necessary.

Even so the really big questions are not answered. What is doing research for a doctorate actually like? How is the decision of what to research actually made? Unlike the natural sciences, the social sciences and humanities do not often provide a situation where the department has ongoing work which requires particular research that a student may follow. Even when something is suggested as fitting the supervisor's own research programme the student may not wish to take it up.

Prospective students apply with very different initial statements of what they hope to do. Some rather vaguely describe a wish to explore some aspect of a phenomenon that interests them but they can't specify exactly what, nor how they would go about it. This is actually a pretty good starting position – a real interest and an open mind. Some want to prove the truth of an opinion they hold. This is trickier since it suggests both an unwillingness to consider other positions and some need for clarification of the idea of proof in research. Yet others write a research plan to a specific hypothesis, setting out methods of research, data collection and analysis. This is also tricky in that interest in the work and appreciation of its proposed significance are not always clear, and in practice few such proposals survive the test of actually carrying them out as proposed. Usually thinking about exactly what to research is either pretty vague or a hazard to fortune at this stage, but it is useful to have a basis for launching an interview with a potential supervisor and it is important to identify a topic or problem that really captures the student's interest and is likely to sustain it through the work for a doctorate. That said, interest may well change in the course of research as the student gets to know the nature of the field and the phenomenon rather better. This is to be expected.

Departments usually arrange a preliminary interview before accepting students. This is a good opportunity for the applicant to ask all those questions they have lined up about any potential supervisor's interest in the application and the way he or she expects to conduct supervision. It is also a good occasion to check on interpretation of documents describing facilities and support within the department as a whole. After such an interview the prospective researcher will have identified some of the features of the job and be better placed to decide whether or not to take it should it be offered – far wiser than starting without first finding out something of where the enjoyments and possible problems might lie.

GETTING STARTED

To change the metaphor, much is now done to make the experience of working for a doctorate one of long-distance running in company rather than lone endeavour, though the persistent 'loner' can still be found and loneliness can be an attitude of mind even when running in company. It is doubtful whether the London marathon works as a model, but the analogy holds quite well. Fellow runners (other researchers), starters (registrars), support teams (departmental staff and facilities), prepared routes (academic custom and practice), finishing lines (successful examination) and completion rites (award of degree and celebration) can all be identified as elements in the analogy. A successful run depends on extending good preparation into getting to know and use fellow runners, support teams and prepared routes throughout the run itself. Just as in the marathon there are different starting points and times for experts and novices, so institutional regulations and practices provide somewhat different routes for differently qualified students. Fast track provision may excuse a student with strong prior experience of research in the relevant field from some of the course requirements and progress reviews which have been set up for those with a lesser proven record, but all have to learn to work with the people and facilities in their department. All that was read in the prospectus and talked about at interview has to become reality in daily work.

Most departments make arrangements for students to learn to use local library and computing facilities, and where appropriate to learn more about typical research sites. These may be regarded as an introduction to essential equipment for work. Getting locked into personal use of computing facilities for data display and analysis, for word-processing, and for desk-top publishing is a first step towards thesis production. It doesn't much matter what is produced at first; the important thing is to have confidence in using the equipment and knowing what to do when it 'plays up'. If necessary it is much better to acknowledge being a beginner, and to demand beginner treatment at the start of the course, than to leave it to a later point of more desperate need.

Equally important is getting to know and use the lay-out, contents and computerized records and procedures of the local library or libraries. These may be regarded as vital sources for at least two kinds of material for research. One is documents as sources of data for use in the research, whilst the other is the published ideas, techniques and findings of other researchers. Any doctoral work can only be assessed as a contribution to knowledge when looked at against this backcloth. Getting to know the backcloth for one's own topic can scarcely be started too soon.

Fellow runners along the route of the research are those local researchers, including other doctoral students, currently working in the field. Starting to find out where they are and what they are doing is a useful move, and guidance may be found from a supervisor or other interested member of staff in the department. Writing to authors who have recently published their own work may yield information about their current work or that of others they happen to know of. Attending conferences can also yield useful contacts.

Starting and continuing to use people in this way is as important as using the material instruments of research. New ideas and techniques come from using mental and technical skills in communities which value them and are producing them. In the research process the ongoing activities of others are prompts for the development of one's own work. This is what library search, correspondence with researchers, supervision practices and research seminars are all about. Right from the beginning it is important to start talking with others about ideas for research and to look for what they have to say.

Since the process of clarifying and developing an actual project usually takes some time it is important to establish a suitable and productive work schedule. Departments usually provide some structure from taught courses, especially in the first year and in the kind of research methods usually found in the relevant field or discipline. Attendance at the whole is expected, and it is a mistake for students to think that only those parts that appear to be of most concern to themselves are worth bothering with. Their own work is usually too embryonic for any certainty about method, and to start with a method preference rather than a good grounding from which to select appropriately when the research question is better formulated is courting trouble. It is usually possible to attend any elements which prove to be most relevant for a particular project or piece of work in a subsequent delivery of the course. Another advantage to learning about a range of methods is the value for understanding the research literature.

For each student, however, a personal plan of work is necessary if action is to be maintained. It is essential to agree a timetable for meetings with supervisors and to sketch out a strategy for preliminary work. It is also helpful to make provisional plans for allocating time to empirical work, or to its equivalent in terms of gathering evidence, particularly if this is to be carried out away from the department. It will be necessary to reserve time at the end for producing the final form of the thesis for submission for examination. Note might be made of when formal reviews of progress may be required or expected by research committees appointed to oversee the development of the work. Such outline planning can only be tentative at first and has to be informed by supervisors' experience in the domain concerned, but knowing that the whole route to the finish is being kept in mind can be very reassuring and is necessary if the work is to be completed in a reasonable time.

MOVING FORWARD

Although some doctoral courses include assessed taught courses, involvement in the research process is the heart of the work of producing a thesis and will therefore be the focus for the rest of this chapter. Many students find the prospect daunting no matter how enthusiastic and excited they are to be starting. It seems to be so difficult to engage with something not really formulated. What is a thesis? The answer to this question depends in part on the customs and practices of the various disciplines, but there are certain features in common which are important structural principles never to be forgotten throughout the work. A thesis is essentially an argument concerning the nature of a phenomenon, an argument that is designed to persuade others that the proposed conclusions have been validly supported and are better argued for than any other proposals.

For example it might be a thesis on the work of an author which offers a new way of looking at it that adds to understanding and appreciation of it. Similarly it may be a thesis on some ethical issue which claims to illuminate some aspect not previously analysed in this way. Or it may be an evaluation of some provision in health, social or educational services which claims to throw new light on problems or outcomes. Or it may be an argument about appropriate instrumentation for tackling some task, offering a newly tested tool for the purpose.

The aim for the researcher at this stage is thus to find a promising area of uncertainty and to set about analysing it and proposing a way forward to try to reduce it. Suggested proposals or topics of interest offered on applying to the department need to be looked at in this light. Tentative research questions may be formulated, not to be set up immediately in terms of method of investigation but in terms of finding out what the present state of play in the field looks like with regard to the issue of uncertainty. Is something new needed or can something new be offered in relation to any existing research programme, any understanding of a problem, any theoretical formulation, any practice in the field, or any way of carrying out investigations?

There are two ways of going about this – discussion with others who are knowledgable in the field and can point in useful directions, and thorough review of the research literature bearing on the area of interest. This will not be the review reported in the final version of the thesis, though it will contain essential material for that review. The review process during the research will be broader and have the character of seeking problems and methods of working on them rather than telling how the literature actually informs the final work. Literature search is helped these days by the computerized services of libraries, but it is well to bear in mind that work of value which was carried out before the days of such services may not be found through them. It helps to read published articles carefully to check on possible use of older sources. But the search should always be governed by questions of what uncertainties are being uncovered and what techniques have been used in work relating to them. This is the obverse of the search for the known which characterises much taught course work, and is characteristic of the research attitude. Sticking to the search for uncertainty can help to avoid an almost un-manageable accumulation of notes which does nothing more than tell the story of the field as it is rather than as it might be. Of course it is important to get to know that story, but it is not essential to write it all down in detail!

The struggle for focus should not be underestimated. It is not easy to combine a good research topic with originality *and* with a scope which is contained sufficiently to be a feasible enterprise for a doctorate. After all there may be very good reasons why there seems to be a particular uncertainty in the literature, not the least being difficulty of access to material or people and possibly related ethical issues. There is at least one university which very firmly advises doctoral students that, since successful theses are publicly available, they should be careful not to use sources or material that may put the welfare or lives of their informants at risk. On other possible matters for concern, professional and learned societies publish ethical codes for researchers covering matters of the treatment of persons and the need to obtain consent from responsible agents and authorities. Quite early in discussions with supervisors it becomes apparent what kind of contribution the student hopes to make to knowledge. Adding to theoretical knowledge is but one kind of work. Equally valuable is the clarification of uncertainties in practical or professional fields or the development of a new instrument or product to the point where it is tested sufficiently to be offered for use by others. Also valuable are new critical insights into published work, new critical biography, or new conceptual analysis. Some disciplines value one kind more than others, but some fields look to a broader coverage. Expectations in a field are important because publication and the views of examiners who are experts in that field need to be thought about. When it is clear to both student and supervisor what kind of work is to be attempted then scope for misunderstanding is much reduced.

DEVELOPING AN ARGUMENT

Advice to research students often moves from considerations of working towards a focused topic to developing one or more research questions. In empirical social sciences in particular these are formulated to carry ways of dealing with evidence to answer the question, which is why the next move is usually to consider research methods. But what implicitly lies behind all this is a point of wider generality for research, applying also to non-empirical work and to the humanities – not to mention the natural sciences! Reliance on method without evaluating its use for a piece of work is likely to lead to the problem of a critic or examiner finding holes in the argument because the nature of the thinking behind the work can get forgotten. What relates research to the topic or problem under investigation is a research argument.

An argument is essentially an example of rational and logical thinking about belief in a proposition. To persuade the research community that any proposition should count as an addition to knowledge it is necessary to assemble and evaluate the evidence used to support it and to consider it against plausible alternatives. This is the essence of research in any discipline, though the nature of the propositions and the evidence varies across disciplines, as do the procedures used to assemble and evaluate both evidence and alternative propositions.

An argument is basically worked around issues which arise in developing thinking about a topic. A fruitful way of bringing these to the surface is to ask questions. What does the topic look like from other perspectives? What possible perspectives might there be? What might happen that I haven't thought about? What do I do if things turn out differently from expected? Can I find better sources or data than those I have so far, and in what sense could they be better? What do I think is the best use to be made of what I am proposing, and where will it not be useful? All such questions carry implications of comparison of some kind, of weighing up or evaluating the quality of sources and evidence, and of comparing possible ways of using information to draw conclusions. In the end a thesis has to be a well-grounded argument which is defensible in public and where limits and shortcomings are recognized – hopefully not as faults but as indications of where some further work might usefully be done.

It may be that an argument turns out to be more complex than some of the literature on research methods suggests. It can certainly be more than that entailed in carrying out a single experiment or a survey or a case study, or, in the non-empirical field, in analysing a single concept or piece of work. Considering possible alternatives may include reports of work already in the literature, but it may also demand formulating and testing such alternatives as part of the work. In experimental studies this may require comparison of the effects of different 'treatments' either in a complex design or in a sequence of studies that logically deals with necessary comparisons. In non-empirical work it may also entail dealing with elements of a complex structure of concepts or events. Not infrequently this means the use of different methods of enquiry and different kinds of data or evidence to deal with different parts of the argument.

It is rarely the case that the structure of an argument can be perceived and held from beginning to end of the research process. It is usually something to be worked out in the process of trying to clarify or reduce the identified uncertainty in the field. For this reason it is unwise to confuse the process with the final thesis, trying to match it with the conventional sequence of sections of a submitted thesis. Rather the expectation should be one of interaction between literature search and review, formulating aims, and working out ways of deciding what evidence is needed and how to obtain it and ensure its reliability and suitability for the task. Such interaction has been described as a cyclical rather than a linear process (Rudestam and Newton, 1992) but whilst this is a useful reminder of the process of refining or changing work as a result of experience, it too may be over simple. What is needed is continuous work on all fronts, adapting and developing where needed in the light of what is found. The research process is more like producing a work of art than following a prescription.

GETTING ON WITH THE WORK

Developing a research design means turning the uncertainty identified as the main target into a manageable problem or set of problems to be solved. There is often more than one way of doing this, and an important aspect of the work is setting up possibilities and then selecting one which can be reasonably defended as better in some way than the others when it comes to writing the thesis. Designs usually involve explicit or implicit comparison between what is already known and what is proposed as new, and it can be quite surprising to find out how much of the logic behind the design of experiments also lies behind making other kinds of comparison and drawing conclusions from them. Research design follows logically from argument, whatever the discipline, so the researcher's prime motto at every point is 'Think straight'. This underpins 'Do it well'.

Most designs are based on a set of simple questions which, taken together in some specified relationship, throw light on the uncertainty at issue. However, it is often the case that one or more of these questions turns out to be more complex than anticipated, in which case it may be sensible to rejig the design to cut out some of the originally planned work. Sometimes the accidents and unanticipated difficulties of one approach may result in change of plan quite some way into the work, and this is much easier to do if the original design was thought through as an informed choice.

Although there is some relief in feeling that the task of settling on a project is becoming clearer, students often feel some disappointment in the reduction of the scope of their interest which is usually necessary for the work itself to be manageable in the time expected. However, it is a useful lesson to learn that research proceeds by small steps and to come to experience something of the reasons for this state of affairs.

Implementing a research design means collecting reliable and apt or appropriate data to inform the argument, and then analysing it accordingly. This raises many of the practical and ethical problems encountered by doctoral students. What kind of information? How best to obtain it? How much? From what sources? Under what conditions?

According to the discipline and research topic, information will be sought from three major kinds of source – people, documents and texts. Research handbooks and textbooks on methods are replete with explanation of various techniques and tools, with guidance for their construction and use. It would be inappropriate to attempt to summarize them here, but some general comments relating to the social sciences in particular may be in order. Techniques such as interview, questionnaire, case study, measurement, observation, discourse analysis, content analysis, etc. are probably best seen as methods in a minor sense, not to be confused with the major sense of developmental, experimental, survey, ethnographic, comparative, phenomenological and hermeneutic methods within which the various techniques are deployed. It is easy to see, for example, that interviewing may serve more than one kind of research method in the major sense, but that it will be designed and carried out very differently if it is supplementing a survey rather than informing an ethnographer. Measuring instruments such as standardized tests, attitude scales, etc. are tools of a rather particular kind, and their use is best seen as method or technique in the minor sense.

This distinction between *major* and *minor* may help to deal with a problem often faced by students today when they meet a distinction between qualitative and quantitative methods without appreciating that it can operate at more than one level. In one sense it refers to major aspects of research, perhaps better termed approach, where a distinction between the search for objectively described attributes can be contrasted with the search for subjective meaning. In another sense it refers to the nature of the information used in research, contrasting numeric with non-numeric representation. It is important to treat the two levels carefully, since although numeric data are associated with the search for objective description, non-numeric may be associated with both objective and subjective attribution. It is even more important not to confuse data with method, since most of the major methods listed above can equally well be associated with either numeric or non-numeric data.

Whilst the research literature reports these various techniques and tools in use, it may be that nothing seems to be entirely appropriate for a particular piece of research. It is therefore incumbent on students to consider whether in making a choice for the purposes of answering their own research questions they may use a tool or technique in a form already tried, or whether they need to develop and test their own. To do this may take time and effort which detracts from the amount of work for which the tool is to be used, but if it is necessary to develop it then to do it well is to advance knowledge. Sometimes a compromise can be worked out in which a standardized test is extended and the product evaluated in the light of findings from the standardized section, but it is not wise to change a test or scale without a fresh standardization. This is not to say, however, that items from a scale may not be used as tasks in an experimental study where they are particularly useful for the question at issue and where adequate design of the experiment obviates the need for standardized measures.

Care with instrumentation, choosing or making the tool to fit the purpose, cannot be overemphasized, whether this be the design and conduct of an interview, the task for an experiment, a questionnaire, a test, or a document or text search. No amount of careful data analysis can compensate for poor quality data, so there is an obligation on any researcher to let the reader of his or her work know what weight can be put on the evidence to be analysed in making the research argument. The information used must be reliably obtained and faithful to its source. The concepts of reliability and validity have a place in non-numeric as well as numeric data gathering, and it is worth spending time discussing and writing down the thinking and piloting behind the data collection for the thesis, for this is part of the defence of the work. Piloting tools and techniques is as important as piloting the procedures of data gathering.

The research itself may require piloting for a number of reasons, largely to do with argument, feasibility or ethics. The 'what if' aspect of an argument requires practical testing, as well as literature-informed thought, in order to avoid an unproductive or inconclusive principal line of research. Sometimes such work is best regarded as an essential first step in an argument rather than a cautious testing, but in either case it should be clearly worked out and written as part of the work to be reported in the thesis. Its effect on the carrying out of the principal or subsequent research can then be spelled out.

Finding that a proposed line of research is not feasible for some unanticipated reason can be very disheartening, unless it can be turned to advantage in reformulating the research argument. Much disappointment can be avoided, however, if adequate thought and enquiry has been given from the start to questions of access to sources of information and to possession of relevant training or experience in working from that source. In education, for example, a study may fall if access to the targeted age group or schools is denied or if the researcher has no experience of the educational system or of working with pupils of the targeted age. Similar considerations apply in anthropology, and it is not stretching the point too far to say that they can also apply to access to and use of documents or texts as data sources. The proposed research must therefore be accommodated to the constraints of access and the ability of the researcher to make the most of the data sources.

Other questions of feasibility are raised by the proposed size of a project. However appealing a proposal to investigate development over time might be, the time limit for doctoral research cannot exceed two years if completion is to be achieved in three or even four. Similarly a project requiring the collection of a large amount of data may be just too large for one researcher, unless he or she is in the fortunate position of being able to use a data source or collection system which effectively extends the work without placing it all on his or her own shoulders. In such cases of 'delegation' care is needed to ensure that it is clear that the thesis is the researcher's own. In general the constraints of time and scope which operate with doctoral research limit the argument, in that trends and generalizations become difficult to deal with.

Ethical issues are also constraining. They centre particularly around improper use of data sources, whether persons, documents or texts. Simple respect for persons should lead to dealing as fully as possible with informed consent to providing data, especially from appropriate adults as well as any children concerned. This is in practice not always an easy matter, not least in deciding what 'informed' means. For example, parents might be quite happy to consent to their children having a particular form of instruction after it has been described to them, but not if it means missing another form which also looks good. With regard to experimental work, the degree to which people are told what is being done may affect how they deal with the task itself, and even their subsequent estimate of their own capabilities. It is probably quite useful in research training to have students experience what it is like to be on the receiving end of a researcher's inconsiderate administration of an experimental task, and to appreciate the importance of both task instruction and later 'debriefing'.

The improper use of documented or text sources is prevented to some extent by careful protection by custodians of such material and by the data protection law, but there is a very grey area concerning the use of material which is the result of the work of others and especially when it is incorporated in a thesis without proper consent or acknowledgement of the source. This may amount to theft of another's work, whether intentional or not, with related problems of deception of examiners and the public, or it may be a case of representing the thinking of another as if it were one's own. The wise researcher develops good habits of source attribution (appropriate to the discipline concerned) in order to avoid inadvertently risking appearing to do this.

Supposing that the work has progressed beyond piloting to the point of assembling the information required for the research argument, and that the researcher is able to defend its suitability and quality for the argument, then comes the task of dealing with it to see how the argument pans out. In empirical studies this takes the form of data analysis in accordance with the research design behind the argument. This is analogous to the way information is drawn on to support or refute propositions in non-empirical work.

For empirical work in the social sciences volumes have been written on the way numeric data can be handled for various kinds of research designs; and research training courses tend to place a great deal of weight on methods of analysis. Dealing with qualitative data is becoming similarly well-established, though more so for approaches which treat data as objective information. There is a different literature on dealing with subjective data gleaned in attempts to probe the meanings of personal or social phenomena to the participants. It tends to address general issues of epistemology whilst accumulating examples of work in the genre. It is clearly impossible in this chapter to deal with data analysis except to indicate its place in the research process.

The crucial issue for the doctoral researcher is to settle for what seems to be the best way to deal with the questions entailed in the research argument. It can be enormously helpful to imagine or take a small subset of the data and set it out in terms of the variables or constructs or ideas it represents, arranging it in ways that bring out the possible relationships to be investigated under the research questions. The very worst thing to do is to enter the data into a computer without its prior organization and the determination of possible analyses. Again, 'What if?' questions are useful, thinking how much easier it would be to instruct a program to omit certain variables, or to treat them in a particular order, or to combine them in some way, if they were readily accessible for such treatment. All this is part of the basic requirement to think clearly.

Such thinking helps the researcher to report the work in a well-formed manner, not obscuring the findings with details which are best filed and made available separately. In the case of a thesis this is usually in an appendix. Such reporting will lead to clear answers to research questions and a good position for relating them in the argument as a whole. It will also allow the researcher to evaluate how well his or her thesis stands up in the light of the evidence and to relate the findings to the purpose of the work.

With the view of research process as outlined here, a development based on continually defining and redefining the argument behind the offering of some new knowledge where a significant uncertainty has been discerned, it comes as no surprise that the final formulation of the argument is captured in writing the thesis. This is not a collection of work written during the research, although it is based on it. It is certainly not a story of the work as it progressed through time, but is a report of the overall outcome. As such it draws on what has been written as the work has progressed, selecting some parts and rejecting others, expanding some and reducing others, all the while focusing on laying out the work to make the argument well.

REVIEWING PROGRESS

It may seem strange that this section has been left to the last, but there is a reason. The final step in producing a thesis is submitting it for examination, a process experienced by the student largely through the oral examination. This is the last of the series of review experiences during the overall research process. It requires the student to demonstrate a good grasp of knowledge in the field and to defend the work reported in the thesis and may itself result in suggestions for further improvement or refinement. Looked at in this way it is obvious that some of the earlier reviewing should have built up experience appropriate for facing an oral examination.

Informal reviewing of progress may take place at any time. It is a built-in aspect of good supervision, as a form of monitoring and as discussion of both the satisfactory and the problematic features of the developing work as seen by both supervisor and student. Special attention to review can result from unexpected hitches or findings or from a sense of losing the thread. There are also 'natural' points when completion of planned sections of work opens up the next moves, and it is often helpful to take an overview of the work when a student is feeling disheartened or is wondering whether or not to continue.

Review is also a feature of good departmental practice where students are expected to present reports of their ongoing work to fellow students and staff. The spirit of review is crucial for the development of the work. Criticism without support for thinking a way through can be very destructive, whilst learning how to meet well-meant and constructive criticism is good training for defending a thesis both in its text and in oral examination. It scarcely matters at what point review is attempted as long as students are helped to relate their work to the literature and to the professional or practical problems in the field, and as long as they are helped to develop and defend a sound way of tackling the gathering and use of relevant and good quality information in their work. Discussion of possible alternative ways of seeing or doing things is really valuable. The same is true of formal review which is usually undertaken at specified points in order to formally advise on the basis of continuing with the work – or even on whether it is wise to carry on. It is sometimes difficult for a committee to remember its advisory role and to refrain from acting as an examining committee but every effort should be made to avoid treating ongoing work as if it were thought to be a completed or even a strong indicator of how the final thesis will shape up. The aim of formal review is to assess the quality of the research so far and the likelihood of it becoming an original and substantial piece of work fit for submission for the ultimate attention of external examiners in the field.

Review as an integral feature of the research process may thus play a critical role. It helps to ensure that the thesis is presented as having a purpose, aims to serve that purpose, roots in existing knowledge, and a defensible method (or methods) of investigation or production that pursues the aims and is designed to yield results which are well-founded and resistant to objection as to their truth, illuminating power or practical utility. If this sounds rather grand, so be it. The successful doctoral researcher has come through an experience that is worthy of respect. The more the work meets these characteristics the greater the deserved respect.

REFERENCES

Eggleston, J. and Delamont, S. (1983) *Supervision of Students for Research Degrees*, British Educational Research Association.

Hampson, L. (1994) *How's Your Dissertation Going? Innovation in Higher Education Series*, Lancaster: Lancaster University.

Noble, K. A. (1994) *Changing Doctoral Degrees: An International Perspective*, Milton Keynes: Society for Research in Higher Education and The Open University Press.

Rudestam, K. E. and Newton, R. R. (1992) *Surviving Your Dissertation: A Comprehensive Guide to Content and Process*, London: Sage Publications.

Chapter 3

Financing a doctorate

Anne Sims

INTRODUCTION

Postgraduate student numbers have increased substantially in recent years as the expansion in undergraduate numbers has led to an increase in demand for postgraduate qualifications. In 1994–5 there were 127,500 full-time postgraduate students in the UK of which 32,800 (26 per cent) were full-time doctoral students (Higher Education Statistics Agency 1995: Table 1). In England, the total number of postgraduate students increased by 85 per cent between 1990 and 1995 (Department for Education News 1995: Table 1).

Unlike undergraduate courses, there is no statutory entitlement to financial support for postgraduate study (with the exception of initial courses of teacher training which attract mandatory awards and student loans). Postgraduate awards are made by selection and, as demand far outstrips supply, competition is now fierce.

The number of awards for postgraduate study has declined sharply in recent years relative to the number of applicants. Indeed, in the academic year 1993–4, only 22 per cent of postgraduate students in the UK held awards (Forth 1995). In 1995 there were 1,680 applicants for Economic and Social Research Council (ESRC) research studentships, yet only 483 awards were available. There were a similar number of applicants for Humanities Research Board (British Academy) research studentships in 1995 – 1,870 – yet only 521 awards were allocated. The success rate for humanities and social science applicants for studentships to undertake doctoral research is therefore 28 per cent (roughly one in four). As competition for postgraduate awards is now very intense, the vast majority of doctoral students clearly cannot be financed by research council awards. Indeed, the decline in the number of awards available at the same time as an enormous increase in demand for postgraduate study has led to the appearance of other avenues for pursuing doctoral research. For example, many institutions now offer research assistant and graduate teaching assistant posts, which aim to attract post-graduate students wishing to pursue doctoral research. The advantages and disadvantages of these routes to obtaining a PhD will be considered in this chapter alongside research council and institutional studentships/bursaries.

Starting life as a postgraduate student is likely to necessitate carrying a continuing burden of debt incurred as an undergraduate. The shift from mandatory grant to loan has resulted in students graduating with increasingly high student loan debts. It has been estimated that students who complete a three-year first degree course in 1998 will owe £4,943 in student loan debt (CVCP 1996: 3). Graduates can defer repayment of student loans if their income is 85 per cent or less of national average earnings and although the loan is index-linked there is a zero rate of real interest. However, for the doctoral student spending perhaps three or four years engaged in further full-time study, the loan debt will obviously continue to accrue during this period.

A review of postgraduate education, conducted by the Higher Education Funding Council for England (HEFCE), the Committee of Vice-Chancellors and Principals (CVCP) and the Standing Conference of Principals (SCOP), was announced in June 1995. The final report is expected to make recommendations on postgraduate funding and support. At the time of writing, the review body's report is awaiting publication.

RESEARCH COUNCIL STUDENTSHIPS

A prospective postgraduate student considering embarking upon a PhD in the social sciences or humanities will probably want first of all to investigate the possibility of obtaining a studentship from one of the research councils which provide financial support for post-graduates.

In April 1994, the research councils were reorganized and seven councils replaced the previous six; between them they cover all fields of academic inquiry. The Economic and Social Research Council (ESRC) covers the social sciences and the Humanities Research Board (HRB) of the British Academy covers humanities (the term 'research council' is used throughout this chapter to refer to both the ESRC and the HRB). The academic subject areas covered by each are listed below.

Economic and Social Research Council (ESRC):

Area Studies	Multidisciplinary Research
Criminology	Planning
Cultural Studies	Politics and International Relations
Economic and Social History	Psychology
Economics	Social Anthropology
Education	Social Policy
Human Geography	Socio-Legal Studies
Industrial Relations	Sociology
Linguistics	Statistics, Research Methods and
Management and Business	Computing Allied to Social
Studies	Sciences
Media Studies	Women's Studies

British Academy – Humanities Research Board (HRB):

Archaeology	Law
Classics	Linguistics
Drama and Theatre Studies	Modern Languages
English	Music
Film Studies	Philosophy
History	Theology
History of Art and Architecture	

Applicants are not permitted to apply to more than one award-making body for support for a particular PhD. Where the proposed field of study is borderline between the social sciences and humanities, applicants are advised to contact either the ESRC or HRB before *15 March* in the year in which the application is to be submitted for advice as to where to apply. It should also be noted that the research councils make awards for academic study and not for courses of vocational or professional training. Awards for such courses, including studentships for research leading to a higher degree in librarianship or information science, are available from the Department for Education and Employment (DfEE). A postgraduate studentship from either the ESRC or the HRB must usually be held at a UK institution.

Full-time and part-time study

Postgraduate studentships from the ESRC or HRB are available for either full-time or part-time study. Full-time research studentships cover fees and maintenance and are usually for three years. Part-time research studentships cover fees plus a limited contribution towards the student's research expenses; they normally last for a maximum of five years. It is possible to transfer between full-time and part-time modes of study.

Eligibility

There are two eligibility conditions: an *academic* requirement and a *residence* requirement. The academic requirement is normally to be a graduate (or prospective graduate) with at least a first or upper second class honours degree from a UK higher education institution. However, it should be stressed that this is a minimum requirement and, as indicated above, being in possession of a first class honours degree does not in itself guarantee an award. Students who have prior experience of postgraduate study are more likely to gain an award than those who do not.

The residence requirement is similar to that for undergraduate (mandatory) awards. However, it differs slightly between the ESRC and HRB. For ESRC awards, the applicant will need to have been ordinarily resident in Great Britain or Northern Ireland for three years immediately preceding the date of application. For HRB awards, applicants need to have been ordinarily resident for three years in England, Wales or Northern Ireland. Those resident in Scotland should apply to the Student Awards Agency Scotland rather than the British Academy for a studentship to study an arts or humanities subject. Residents of the Channel Islands and the Isle of Man should apply to their respective island authorities (see contact addresses at the end of this chapter).

To qualify as 'ordinarily resident' the applicant should not have been resident during any part of the three year period wholly or mainly for the purpose of receiving full-time education. Temporary absences abroad need not break a period of ordinary residence.

Those recognized as refugees, granted asylum or European Union (EU) nationals who have 'migrant worker' status are exempted from the ordinary residence requirement. EU nationals who do not have 'migrant worker' status and who do not meet the ordinary residence requirement can apply for a 'fees-only' award, provided they have been resident in a European Economic Area (EEA) country for three years immediately preceding the application. A 'fees-only' award covers tuition fees but no payments are made in respect of maintenance (see research council handbooks for further details of residence requirements).

Making an application for a research studentship

ESRC studentships

Those seeking an ESRC studentship should check whether the institution/department has been approved by the ESRC for receipt of its awards; not all institutions receive such approval. A list is available annually from the ESRC: *Institutions, Departments/Outlets and Programmes Approved for the Receipt of ESRC Research Studentships*. The applicant must be nominated by the department where s/he wishes to study. Thus the applicant must first be accepted by the department before applying for an award.

There are two modes of ESRC recognition: A and B. Departments which have Mode A recognition provide research training to students in their first year; Mode A departments can therefore accept students who do not have any previous research experience. Departments with Mode B recognition can only accept students with previous research training, such as a master's degree which includes research methods or the first year of a PhD programme elsewhere. The applicant should therefore check carefully whether the department can accept her/him before making an application.

The ESRC also has a small number of collaborative research (CASE) studentships linked with either businesses or the public/ voluntary sector. These are allocated to academic departments and employers on a quota basis. Collaborative research students receive an allowance from the collaborating partner in addition to the maintenance grant by the ESRC. Applicants who are interested in a CASE studentship should ask the academic department whether it has an ESRC quota. A list of departments holding quotas is available from the ESRC every year.

HRB studentships

Applicants for an HRB studentship should note that they may apply either for a Competition A (one-year) or a Competition B (three-year) studentship. Those wishing to undertake doctoral research may apply in the first instance for a Competition A award; however, the programme of research must be a 'coherent project in itself'. After the first year, the student can compete for a Competition B studentship, although there is no guarantee that receipt of a one-year award – and successful completion of the programme of study – will lead to a subsequent three-year studentship.

Undergraduates or those with no experience of postgraduate study should give careful consideration to whether to apply for a Competition A studentship or for both Competitions A and B simultaneously rather than proceeding straight to an application for a three-year studentship. The vast majority of Competition B awards go to those who already have experience of postgraduate study. Furthermore, it is not possible to extend a Competition B studentship beyond three years (or five years part time).

In 1996 the HRB introduced a scheme of awards made in partnership with institutions ('partnership awards'). The aim of the scheme is to offer awards to doctoral students to contribute towards research which is already ongoing in an institution. Institutions are expected to meet half the costs of the award. There is no separate quota of awards under this scheme and applicants are assessed competitively alongside those for conventional awards.

Submitting the application

In respect of both ESRC and HRB awards, applicants should submit an application on the prescribed form, through the institution where they intend to study. *Applications are always made via the department where the student has applied to study rather than directly to the research council.* The deadline for both ESRC and HRB awards is 1 May. This deadline is strictly adhered to and applications will not be accepted after this date. Faxed applications are not acceptable. Proof of posting (obtainable from the Post Office) is advised in the event of dispute over a lost or delayed application.

When the applicant has completed the form s/he must pass it on to two referees to write testimonials, one of whom should normally be the applicant's undergraduate tutor. It is then the responsibility of the institution to ensure that the application form is returned to the ESRC or HRB. It is therefore important that the candidate allows ample time for references to be completed and the form returned by the deadline of 1 May. In practice this is likely to mean that candidates will need to have been offered a place and to have completed the relevant application form for a studentship by the *end of March* in order to allow sufficient time for testimonials to be written and the forms to be forwarded to the award-making body by the closing date (refer to the research council handbooks for further information on application procedures).

Selection procedures

Each application is assessed on its merits by a panel of subject experts. The following information is taken into account: the applicant's first degree results; reasons for undertaking the proposed research; aptitude for research/description of project; compatibility of candidate's and department's research interests including the support/facilities the institution is able to provide.

Candidates are usually notified of the outcome of their application by the end of July (for ESRC awards) or during July/August (HRB awards). Those placed on a reserve list will not be informed until September.

Composition of the award

A research studentship from either the ESRC or HRB will differ depending on whether it is held in respect of full-time or part-time study or whether it is a 'fees-only' award. Full value awards (fees and maintenance) are only paid in respect of full-time study. Unlike undergraduate (mandatory) awards, postgraduate studentships are not means-tested against student's, parental or spouse's income. Grant and fee rates are uprated annually – check the relevant handbook for current rates. A 'fees-only' award (full-time or part-time) payable to EU nationals consists of the payment to the institution of tuition fees only.

Part-time studentships consist of:

- tuition fees (pro-rata)
- a small amount (payable to the department) for direct support of the student's research. The student may claim reimbursement for costs arising from fieldwork, essential visits, attendance at conferences and for incidental expenses such as photocopying costs.

Full-time studentships consist of:

- tuition fees – up to set maxima laid down by the DfEE
- maintenance grant – including any additional allowances
- additional expenses (for fieldwork, attendance at conferences, study visits, etc.)

A basic maintenance grant is payable at two rates depending on whether the student is studying at an institution in London or outside London. The maintenance grant covers a 52-week year and is paid quarterly in advance, via the institution. Studentships normally commence at the beginning of October.

Applicants should note that daily travel expenses are deemed to be included in the basic maintenance grant. Also, additional expenses cannot be claimed for incidental expenses such as photocopying or for typing or binding a thesis.

The following additional allowances are available:

- Dependants' allowances. These are payable in respect of a dependent spouse and/or children. However, from 1996–7 new award-holders can only claim dependants' allowances in respect of children; it is no longer possible to claim for a spouse. Existing award-holders (i.e. those whose awards commenced prior to 1996–7) can continue to claim for a dependent spouse.
- Disabled students' allowance. This can be claimed by students who are obliged to incur additional expenditure in connection with their studies because of a disability. For further information contact the relevant research council.
- Mature students' incentive. This allowance is paid by the ESRC in respect of students who are aged 26 or over on the 1 September preceding the start of the award. Students who will reach the age of 26 within the duration of the award do not become eligible. The HRB does not pay a mature students' incentive.

Additional expenses are payable to full-time students in receipt of a maintenance grant only; expenses may not be claimed by EU students in receipt of a 'fees-only' award. Additional expenses can be claimed in respect of fieldwork, attendance at conferences and study visits. The ESRC pays an allowance (UK Fieldwork Allowance) to the institution for such expenses, incurred within the UK/EU, in respect of each ESRC-funded research student. Students should therefore claim the expenses from their department. Those in receipt of HRB awards will need to obtain the prior approval of the HRB if they wish to be reimbursed for attendance at conferences or expenses relating to fieldwork (subject to a maximum per student per academic year). The ESRC and the HRB will only contribute to expenses arising from *one* overseas fieldwork trip throughout the duration of the award.

Terms and conditions of the award

Both ESRC and HRB studentships have specific terms and conditions attached to their tenure relating to monitoring of progress, suspension of study/sickness, holidays, employment, transfers and termination of awards. These primarily relate to full-time students. Detailed information is available in the *ESRC Studentship Handbook: A Guide for Postgraduate Award Holders* (1995) and the HRB publication *Guide to Postgraduate Studentships in the Humanities* (1996).

Award-holders should note, in particular, that continuation of the award will be subject to confirmation, annually, of satisfactory progress. An award may be terminated at any time, at the discretion of the ESRC or HRB, if an unsatisfactory report is received or if the student ceases to be engaged in the approved programme of study. Where an award is terminated prematurely for any reason the student will be liable to repay any maintenance grant and/or expenses which have been overpaid.

Students are permitted to take up to eight weeks holiday in twelve months (including public holidays). During periods of certificated sickness the maintenance grant will continue to be paid at the full rate for the first four weeks of sickness and half-rate for the next four weeks during any twelve-month period. Awards are normally suspended when periods of sickness exceed eight weeks.

Full-time award-holders are permitted to undertake teaching duties providing these do not exceed 180 hours per academic year (or six hours per week), *including preparation and marking*. Students are expected to inform the ESRC or HRB if they undertake other types of paid work, either during term or vacation; it is not encouraged. If a full-time student takes up full-time paid employment of any kind, the award will be terminated from the date of the appointment.

INSTITUTIONAL STUDENTSHIPS AND BURSARIES

In addition to research council awards, many universities themselves offer studentships or bursaries. These are usually advertised and are therefore subject to open competition. The number of awards held by a university (or department) is often small and may be limited to a narrow range of disciplines. Furthermore, studentships may attach to specific research projects so that applicants may be limited in their choice of research topic.

Although eligibility requirements are often similar to those attached to research council awards, terms and conditions vary enormously. In many instances, fees are waived and the maintenance element payable is comparable with research council rates. In some cases, however, the studentship may be 'fees-only' and possibly part-time.

Some institutional studentships or bursaries are open to overseas students – although fee remission may be at the home rate so that students who are liable for overseas fees will be required to make up the difference. It is particularly important to check whether teaching duties are a condition of tenure of the studentship and, if so, the number of hours, pay and nature of the teaching required (for more on teaching duties see under 'Employment' below).

Institutional studentships are advertised in the education press (the *Guardian, Independent, Times Higher Education Supplement*) early in the year with closing dates often in February or March. The *Times Higher Education Supplement* produces a listing, 'Research Opportunities', three times a year (in February, May and September). This lists research degrees by subject across UK institutions and also the availability of funding. Alternatively, applicants can approach the department where they wish to study with a research proposal and enquire whether any studentships may be available.

EMPLOYMENT

Students undertaking doctoral research may be employed by an institution either as research assistants, teaching assistants or as casual teaching staff. By offering potential postgraduate students employment as teachers or researchers universities can attract those wishing to register for a higher degree who would not otherwise be able to finance further study. In practice, it may be much easier to secure one of these positions than to obtain a research council award.

Research assistant posts

These posts are well-established and can be a useful way of pursuing a PhD whilst undertaking research for the institution as a salaried staff member. Choice of research topic will, however, be circumscribed and the research assistant may be required to contribute to a number of areas of research in the department; s/he may also be expected to undertake teaching duties. The research assistant, therefore, is likely to be able to pursue her/his own research on a part-time basis only. Moreover, as research assistants are often employed on short-term contracts (typically one or two years) it will probably be necessary to secure more than one post in order to complete a PhD.

Although research assistant salaries are higher than research council awards or institutional bursaries, those appointed at pre-doctoral level are usually placed towards the bottom of the scales. In 1995–6, pay scales for research assistants started at £9,462 in 'new' universities and £14,317 in 'old' universities (for information on which are 'new' and 'old' universities, contact the Higher Education Funding Council for England or Wales or the Education Department in Scotland or Northern Ireland).

Research assistant posts are advertised regularly in the education press. Alternatively, those considering pursuing this route to a PhD can write to any academic department requesting a copy of its publications list. If the areas of research match the candidate's own, it may be worth sending a c.v. asking to be informed should any suitable vacancies arise.

Graduate teaching assistant posts

Teaching assistantships have grown in popularity in recent years as universities have required more staff to teach increasing numbers of undergraduates. These posts afford graduates an opportunity to register for a higher degree whilst undertaking paid teaching work in the department on fixed-term, renewable contracts. In return, the postgraduate is offered a bursary – often broadly equivalent to a research council award – and sometimes additional pay for teaching duties; postgraduate fees are waived. Aside from the obvious financial benefits, teaching assistantships offer those wishing to pursue an academic career an opportunity to gain valuable teaching experience.

The growth in graduate teaching assistant posts, however, has attracted criticism. The National Postgraduate Committee, for example, has noted that:

Teaching Assistant posts vary greatly in their terms and conditions, ranging from being a method of increasing research student numbers and providing cheap, low grade, laboratory or tutorial assistance, right through to schemes intended for 'writing-up' or newly graduated postgraduates almost as a full member of teaching staff.

(Irvine and Darwen 1994: 3)

Similarly, lecturers' trade unions have been critical of the scheme because of its potential to exploit postgraduate students whilst diminishing the number of jobs available for those wishing to embark upon an academic career. The university and college lecturers' union, NATFHE, opposes the introduction of teaching assistants and argues that such proposals emanate from 'growing pressure to deliver cheaper teaching'. The union believes that all teaching staff should be employed on lecturer pay scales and conditions of service; employing staff on poor terms and conditions inevitably has a detrimental impact on the quality of education. Indeed, teaching assistants undermine the position of lecturing staff and should be resisted. If the institution offers a postgraduate student a bursary, this should not be conditional upon undertaking unpaid teaching; rather, students should be paid nationally agreed hourly rates (NATFHE 1995a; NATFHE 1995b).

The Association of University Teachers (AUT), on the other hand, is not opposed in principle to graduate teaching assistant schemes. Nevertheless, it is also concerned about the potential of such schemes to exploit postgraduates whilst simultaneously undermining the quality of both undergraduate teaching and postgraduate research. The AUT has drawn up a list of minimum conditions which it believes are acceptable for the employment of graduate teaching assistants. These are summarized below.

- The role of teaching assistants should be limited to *assisting* academic staff (i.e. demonstrating, taking seminars/tutorials, assisting on field trips). Teaching assistants should not, therefore, be involved in lecturing (apart from occasional lectures on topics related to their research field), course design/content or in examining/assessment which affects final degree classification.
- The amount of time that teaching assistants are engaged in teaching related activities should be limited to six contact hours per week during term/semester time; total teaching related hours should be limited to twelve per week or 360 per year.
- Pay should be clearly related to academic salary scales and should consist of a student bursary plus appropriate pay for teaching duties.
- Teaching assistants should be provided with a formal written contract specifying scope/amount of teaching duties; pay should be itemized. Contracts should have a duration of at least four years to allow sufficient time for completion of a PhD.

- Teaching assistants should be exempt from paying registration fees; they should receive expenses for fieldwork and attending conferences in relation to their research, comparable with those which students in receipt of research council awards are eligible to receive.
- Adequate and appropriate training for teaching should be provided as well as adequate supervision from academic staff in respect of the postgraduate's teaching role. Appropriate facilities (office space, access to telephones and photocopying) should also be provided.

(AUT 1993; AUT 1995a)

As the terms and conditions attached to graduate teaching assistant schemes vary considerably, it is important to scrutinize these carefully before accepting a post. Pay, number of required teaching hours, the nature of the teaching/assessment expected and the availability of training are all widely variable. Some universities, for example, have set up formal training schemes for teaching assistants, which include training in teaching, learning and assessment, in recognition of the fact that formal training of graduate teachers benefits both postgraduates and undergraduates alike. Applicants should therefore check the following:

- Pay – are teaching duties a condition of receipt of the bursary or are they paid separately?
- Fees – are PhD fees included? At home/European Union rate only?
- Teaching – how many hours and what are the duties (i.e. lectures, tutorials/seminars, assessment) and subject areas?
- Training – is any training available in teaching and assessment? If so, is it accredited?
- Assessment – is there any formal assessment of the postgraduate's teaching or mechanisms for feedback/evaluation?
- Contract – what is the duration of the contract, is it renewable and subject to what conditions (e.g. satisfactory performance/progress)?

Both NATFHE and the AUT encourage graduate teaching assistants to join their relevant trades union and to seek representation on issues relating to their employment.

In practice, the teaching workload attached to a teaching assistantship is likely to necessitate a longer period for completion of a PhD. The National Postgraduate Committee has noted that in the US, where teaching assistant schemes are well-established, postgraduates working as teaching assistants can take ten years or longer to complete a PhD (Irvine and Darwen 1994: 10).

Casual hourly paid teaching

Hourly paid teaching has traditionally been undertaken by doctoral students, usually involving laboratory/demonstrating or tutorial/seminar work. Teaching is useful not only as a source of income, but for the benefits it brings in terms of experience, personal development and enhanced understanding of the postgraduate's subject area.

Nevertheless, there are concerns that a combination of understaffed academic departments and the shortage of funding for postgraduate study has led to pressure on postgraduates to take on increasingly heavy teaching commitments. This, in turn, can result in the postgraduate's own research suffering and poor teaching quality for undergraduates.

In response to the growth in the use of postgraduates as teachers – and the consequent disparate practices which have emerged – the National Postgraduate Committee has produced a set of guidelines on the employment of postgraduates as teachers. The guidelines attempt to formalize the arrangements for the casual employment of postgraduates and aim to ensure high quality teaching. They are summarized below.

- Teaching should be distributed fairly amongst postgraduate students wishing to undertake this work.
- Full-time research students should not undertake more than 180 hours of teaching per year, *including preparation and marking* (for those in receipt of research council awards this is stipulated in the terms and conditions).
- Postgraduate students who do not wish to teach should not be pressurized into doing so.
- Pay structure should be unambiguous: either teaching is salaried or paid on a properly specified hourly basis.
- A written contract should be issued to all postgraduates engaged in teaching, detailing the following: pay, duties, class contact hours, total number of hours preparation required, marking and any training or administration required.
- All postgraduates involved in teaching should be afforded an opportunity to undertake formal training in teaching skills and

methods and in marking and assessment. Postgraduates should not, however, be expected to mark work which is assessed for the purpose of a student's final degree classification.

- Postgraduate students should undergo prior assessment of their ability to teach.
- Academic departments should nominate a member of staff with responsibility for co-ordinating postgraduate teaching in the department and facilitating feedback.
- Academic departments should provide insurance cover to indemnify postgraduate teachers against legal liability or recommend membership of the recognized trade union for this purpose.
- Suitable accommodation should be provided for postgraduates who are required to carry out individual tuition.

(NPC 1993)

Surveys which have been conducted on postgraduates employed as teachers have highlighted the need for more formalized arrangements. For example, a National Postgraduate Committee survey found that only about one in eight postgraduates engaged in teaching had received any training in how to teach. The same survey found that postgraduates engaged in tutorial/seminar work averaged two hours of preparation and marking for every contact hour – a ratio of total time to contact time of 3:1 (Irvine and Darwen 1994: 2–3). Thus, if those in receipt of research studentships are to remain within the maximum teaching hours stipulated by the research councils (180 per year), this means that they should undertake, on average, no more than *sixty hours of class contact per year, or two hours per week.*

Pay for postgraduates engaged in teaching also varies widely. Postgraduate teachers should be paid at the same rates as other casual, hourly paid teaching staff. This is not always the case; the National Postgraduate Committee has commented that 'postgraduates are being increasingly exploited as teachers, but they are so desperate for the work that they will accept very low rates of pay' (quoted in Sanders 1994).

Pay scales, in fact, differ between 'old' and 'new' university sectors. They are negotiated by the Association of University Teachers (AUT) in the 'old' universities and by the university and college lecturers' union, NATFHE, in the 'new' universities. In the 'old' universities there are no nationally agreed rates of pay for hourly paid teaching staff; the AUT's policy is that the rate for hourly paid staff should be calculated pro-rata, as a fraction of a point on the full-time salary scale. On this basis, the hourly rate of pay for tutorial work (based on the salary scales agreed on 1 April 1995) would be a minimum of £27.55. This calculation assumes two hours of preparation for every contact hour (AUT 1995b). In practice, however, actual rates of pay for postgraduate teachers employed in 'old' universities are much lower. A survey conducted jointly by the AUT, the National Union of Students (NUS) and the National Postgraduate Committee in 1995 found that rates of pay per hour actually worked averaged £3.79 for those engaged in lecturing, £4.40 for those engaged in tutorial work and £6.22 for those involved in demonstrating. The reason for the higher average rate for demonstrating compared with those for lecturing and tutorial work is that *total* hours worked (i.e. including preparation and marking) are fewer (AUT/NUS/NPC 1996).

In the 'new' universities, there are nationally agreed part-time hourly rates negotiated by the lecturers' union, NATFHE. At 1 September 1995 the rate for higher education level work (categories I, II/III) was £23.30 per hour. London weightings are also applicable (per hour):

Inner London £2.03
Outer London £1.34
Fringe £0.51

These rates are subject to annual increases.

Postgraduates engaged in teaching duties are eligible to join an appropriate trade union and should seek advice regarding pay and terms and conditions issues from their local NATFHE or AUT representative.

OTHER SOURCES OF SUPPORT

So far in this chapter, the main sources of funding for doctoral students have been considered: awards/studentships and employment. There are, however, a miscellany of other sources of support which may be appropriate in particular circumstances. These are considered, in brief, below.

Access Funds

These are funds made available to universities by central government for distribution to individual students 'whose access to further or higher education might be inhibited by financial considerations or who, for whatever reason, including physical or other disabilities, face financial difficulties' (HEFCE 1995: para. 9).

There is a separate fund for postgraduates, although in practice universities often merge it with their undergraduate fund. All full-time 'home' students are eligible to apply for assistance from the Access Funds. However, within this broad category of eligibility, universities are free to determine their own criteria for distribution.

The amounts available are limited. Moreover, the range of payments made varies considerably. For example, in 1994–5, the lowest payment made to postgraduates was £2, the highest £7,850, with an average payment of £526 (HEFCE 1996). It is worth noting that this range is outwith Higher Education Funding Council guidance which stipulates a minimum payment of £100 and a maximum payment of £3,000. The guidance also states that Access Funds should *not* be used to fund studentships or postgraduate bursaries.

In practice, nearly one-third of the postgraduate Access Fund is used to finance accommodation costs, whilst 27 per cent is used to assist the payment of fees. The funds are also used to contribute to the costs of travel, childcare and books/equipment (HEFCE 1996).

Doctoral students wishing to apply for assistance from the Access Funds should enquire at the student advice service at their university. However, they should bear in mind that universities often target specific groups such as single parents, students with disabilities, mature students with dependants and self-financing students.

Social Security Benefits

Students engaged in *full-time* study are not usually eligible to claim means-tested benefits (Income Support and Housing Benefit) unless they are in one of a few exempt groups – i.e. single parents, students with disabilities or student couples with dependent children. Social Security regulations stipulate that full-time students are disentitled from claiming benefits from the first day through to the last day of the course (or until the student abandons or is dismissed from the course). Thus, the disentitlement continues during periods of absence – due, for example, to sickness – so long as a full-time student continues to be registered at the university.

However, students who are likely to be sick for a long period should make a claim for Incapacity Benefit and continue to submit medical certificates to the Benefits Agency. Although the student may not qualify for Incapacity Benefit (because s/he does not satisfy the National Insurance contribution conditions), s/he will be eligible to claim Income Support or Housing Benefit after twenty-eight weeks of incapacity due to being classed as a disabled student.

Full-time postgraduate students in receipt of a studentship or award who are eligible to claim means-tested benefits should note that the maintenance element of the award will be treated as income, subject to certain disregards. Where a non-student heterosexual partner makes a claim on behalf of the couple, the student's grant income will also be taken into account. Similarly, earned income is also taken into account subject to a disregard (usually £5 per week).

Part-time students are eligible to claim Housing Benefit. The situation with regard to Income Support is more complicated. From October 1996 only people not required to be available for employment (such as single parents and those who are sick) continue to be eligible for Income Support; those who are registered as unemployed and required to be available for employment are eligible to claim a new benefit, Jobseeker's Allowance.

Those in receipt of Jobseeker's Allowance can study if registered *part-time*. However, it must be stressed that the conditions for receipt of this benefit are strict: claimants are required to be immediately available for and actively seeking employment. It would not therefore be advisable to commence a part-time PhD on the assumption that it will be possible to finance it by this means. Any doubt about the claimant's availability for employment is likely to result in benefit being disallowed. (For further information on students and social security benefits, see CPAG 1996a; NUS 1995b; Finn and Murray 1996.)

Career Development Loans

This is a Department for Education and Employment (DfEE) scheme, operated in partnership with high street banks, whereby loans are available for vocational education or training. Four banks participate in the scheme: Barclays, the Cooperative, Clydesdale and the Royal Bank of Scotland. A Career Development Loan (CDL) can cover up to 80 per cent of course fees; in respect of full-time study, the loan can also cover living expenses. The maximum which can be borrowed is £8,000. Interest is paid by the DfEE whilst study is being undertaken; thereafter the borrower is liable for repayment of the loan plus interest (commercial rates of interest apply). Repayment begins one month after the period of study supported by the CDL has ceased, unless the borrower is unemployed in which case repayment can be deferred for a further five months.

Although any mode and level of study can be supported with a CDL, in practice it is not a usual means of financing a PhD. This is because the study in respect of which the loan is taken out has to be job-related; also, only two years of study can be supported by a Career Development Loan. CDLs are an expensive way of financing study and are only really worth considering if no other sources of finance are available. For further information telephone Freephone 0800 585 505.

OVERSEAS STUDENTS

Overseas students are not eligible to apply for research council awards unless they have been ordinarily resident in the UK for three years (European Union students are eligible to apply for 'fees-only' awards – see under 'Research Council Studentships' above). Unless students from overseas can find some form of scholarship or sponsorship they are liable to pay their own tuition fees. Universities are free to set their own fee levels. In 1995–6 the most common fee level in respect of classroom-based postgraduate research courses was between £5,700 and £6,100 (CVCP 1995a).

There are, however, specific British government schemes for overseas students wishing to undertake postgraduate study in the UK. The main schemes funded by the Overseas Development Administration (ODA) and the Department for Education and Employment (DfEE) are outlined below.

Overseas Research Students Awards Scheme (ORSAS)

This scheme has been in existence since 1979. It is administered by the Committee of Vice-Chancellors and Principals (CVCP) on behalf of the DfEE. About 850 awards are offered annually; they provide partial fee remission only (the difference between the fee for a home postgraduate student and the 'full-cost' fee charged by the university for an overseas student in the relevant field of study). Maintenance costs are not covered. Awards are made on a competitive basis to overseas postgraduate students 'of outstanding merit and research potential' (CVCP 1995b: 3). Nearly 200 institutions in the UK participate in the scheme and awards are offered to students from approximately eighty countries worldwide.

As is the case in respect of all postgraduate awards, competition is now intense; the number of awards available has declined substantially in recent years relative to the number of applicants. Students are not permitted to apply for an award through more than one institution. Awards are made initially for one year but are renewable for a second or third year, subject to satisfactory progress. Further details and application forms are obtainable from the registry of any UK institution participating in the scheme. Enquiries concerning participating institutions should be made to the ORSAS Office, CVCP, 29 Tavistock Square, London, WC1H 9EZ. Telephone: 0171 387 9231.

Commonwealth Scholarship and Fellowship Plan (CSFP)

This is an ODA-funded scheme which assists commonwealth students to study in other commonwealth countries. It aims to promote equality of educational opportunity and contribute to development in Commonwealth countries. It is open to applicants from developing Commonwealth countries of 'high academic calibre' who preferably intend to study a subject of developmental relevance (Foreign and Commonwealth Office 1995: 5). Scholarship awards are available under the scheme for those wishing to pursue postgraduate degrees at UK universities. Applicants should be resident in their own country at the time of application, from whence the application is made.

The CSFP scheme is administered in the UK by the Association of Commonwealth Universities (ACU). Further information and advice on applications is available from the ACU, John Foster House, 36 Gordon Square, London, WC1H 0PF. Telephone: 0171 387 8572.

British Chevening Scholarships

This programme is funded by the Foreign and Commonwealth Office. It aims to attract to the UK able students from countries with whom the UK is expected to develop economic relations. Approximately 3,000 awards are made annually to students from a wide variety of countries.

Scholarships are given for study in any field, but developmental relevance is likely to be an important factor in respect of candidates whose country is a recipient of UK bilateral aid. Awards are available for students wishing to pursue full-time postgraduate research-based courses at UK institutions. Preference is given to those already established in a career. Most scholarships are awarded for one year.

Candidates apply in their own country through the British diplomatic mission. Further information is obtainable from the British Council, Medlock Street, Manchester M15 4PR. Telephone: 0161 957 7298.

British Council Fellowships Programme

This scheme, established in 1985, is funded and administered by the British Council. It is aimed at professionals in fields which the British Council considers important in the relevant country. There are no restrictions on subject of study. About 900 awards are made annually in most of the 100 countries in which the British Council operates.

Awards can be for up to three years' duration and can include studies leading to a PhD. The level and conditions of the award are set by the British Council in each country. However, awards can include fees, living expenses, allowances for books/travel and return fares to the UK.

British Council representatives overseas are responsible for selecting candidates. Applications should be made to the Council Director in the country concerned. Further information is obtainable from The Director, Development and Training Services, The British Council, Medlock Street, Manchester M15 4PR. Telephone: 0161 957 7615/7867.

CONCLUSION

There have been two major changes in student support in recent years which, together, have impacted harshly upon doctoral students. First, financing a doctorate now involves navigating a complex labyrinth of support systems. It is no longer a straightforward matter simply of applying to the relevant research council for a postgraduate studentship: as only about one in four applicants for studentships are successful, the vast majority of prospective doctoral students must necessarily look elsewhere for support. This often involves paid employment of one kind or another.

Second, it is increasingly the case that students wishing to embark upon postgraduate study do so carrying a heavy burden of debt incurred as an undergraduate. Although student loan repayments can be deferred during a period of postgraduate study, interest continues to accrue, creating an incentive for the student to complete her/his doctoral research as quickly as possible in order to start repaying the loan. Paradoxically, however, the imperative to work – in order to be able to pursue doctoral study at all – is likely to lead to a longer completion period during which debt continues to accrue.

CONTACT ADDRESSES

Humanities Research Board
The British Academy
Block 1, Spur 15
Government Buildings
Honeypot Lane
Stanmore, Middlesex
HA7 1AZ
Telephone: 0181 951 5188

Postgraduate Training Division
Economic and Social Research
   Council
Polaris House
North Star Avenue
Swindon, SN2 1UJ
Telephone: 01793 413000

Department for Education and
   Employment
Mowden Hall
Staindrop Road
Darlington, Co. Durham
DL3 9BG
Telephone: 01325 460155

Student Awards Agency Scotland
Gyleview House
Redheughs Rigg
Edinburgh, EH12 9HH
Telephone: 0131 556 8400

Department of Education for
   Northern Ireland
Student Support Branch
Rathgael House
Balloo Road
Bangor, Co. Down
BT19 7PR
Telephone: 01247 279279

Department of Education
Murray House
Mount Havelock
Douglas
Isle of Man
Telephone: 01624 685784

State of Guernsey Education
   Department
PO Box 32, Grange Road
St Peter Port
Guernsey
C.I. GY 3AU
Telephone: 01481 710821

State of Jersey Education
   Committee
PO Box 142, Highlands
St Saviour
Jersey, C.I.
Telephone: 0153 471065

Higher Education Funding
  Council for England
Northavon House
Coldharbour Lane
Bristol, BS16 1QD
Telephone: 0117 9317317

Higher Education Funding
  Council for Wales
Lambourne House
Cardiff Business Park
Llanishen, Cardiff
CF4 5GL
Telephone: 01222 761861

REFERENCES

AUT (1993) *Postgraduate Teaching Assistant Schemes*, LA/4839, London: Association of University Teachers.

AUT (1995a) *Graduate Teaching Assistants*, LA/5588, London: Association of University Teachers.

AUT (1995b) *Part Time not Part Person*, London: Association of University Teachers.

AUT/NUS/NPC (1996) *Survey of Postgraduate Teachers 1995*, London: Association of University Teachers.

CPAG (1996a) *National Welfare Benefits Handbook 1996/97*, London: Child Poverty Action Group Ltd.

CPAG (1996b) *Rights Guide to Non-means-tested Benefits 1996/97*, London: Child Poverty Action Group Ltd.

CVCP (1995a) *Results of Survey of Overseas Students' Tuition Fees for 1995/6*, London: Committee of Vice-Chancellors and Principals.

CVCP (1995b) *Overseas Research Students Awards Scheme: Annual Report 1994–95*, London: Committee of Vice-Chancellors and Principals.

CVCP (1996) *The Government's Student Loans Scheme*, London: Committee of Vice-Chancellors and Principals.

Department for Education News (1995) *Student Enrolments on Higher Education Courses in England and in the United Kingdom: Academic Year 1994–95*, 19 May, London: Department for Education.

ESRC (1995) *ESRC Studentship Handbook 1995: A Guide for Postgraduate Award Holders*, Swindon: Economic and Social Research Council.

ESRC (1996a) *ESRC Research Studentships 1996: Guidance Notes for Applicants*, Swindon: Economic and Social Research Council.

ESRC (1996b) *Institutions, Departments/Outlets and Programmes Approved for the Receipt of ESRC Research Studentships 1996/97*, Swindon: Economic and Social Research Council.

ESRC (1996c) *ESRC Recognition of Training Courses and Programmes - Postgraduate Training Guidelines*, Swindon: Economic and Social Research Council.

Finn, D. and Murray I. (1996) *Unemployment and Training Rights Handbook*, London: Unemployment Unit.

Foreign and Commonwealth Office (1995) *British Government and British Council Award Schemes for Overseas Students and Trainees*, London: Foreign and Commonwealth Office.

Forth, E. (1995) *Hansard*, House of Commons, 17 November, 1995, col. 240.

HEFCE (1995) *Access Funds: 1995–96 Allocation and Terms and Conditions for Payments of Grant*, Bristol: Higher Education Funding Council for England.

HEFCE (1996) *Use of the Access Funds by HEFCE funded Institutions 1994–95*, unpublished, Higher Education Funding Council for England.

Higher Education Statistics Agency (1995) *Data Report – Students in Higher Education Institutions*, Cheltenham: HESA Services Ltd.

Irvine, J. and Darwen, J. (1994) 'The Use of Postgraduate Students as Teachers', paper presented to the Society for Research into Higher Education Annual Conference, York 1994.

NATFHE (1995a) *Lecturers on the Cheap*, London: National Association of Teachers in Further and Higher Education.

NATFHE (1995b) *Teaching Assistants – Oppose Higher Education 'On The Cheap'*, London: National Association of Teachers in Further and Higher Education.

NPC (1993) *Guidelines for the Employment of Postgraduate Students as Teachers*, Troon: National Postgraduate Committee.

NUS (1995a) *Postgraduate Funding*, London: National Union of Students.

NUS (1995b) *Social Security Benefits*, London: National Union of Students.

Sanders, C. (1994) 'Pay cut for desperate postgrads', *Times Higher Education Supplement*, 28 January.

The British Academy: Humanities Research Board (1996) *Guide to Postgraduate Studentships in the Humanities 1996*, Stanmore: The British Academy, Humanities Research Board.

Chapter 4

Planning time

Derek May

INTRODUCTION: THE TIME THAT HAS TO BE PLANNED

University regulations are more likely to specify a minimum rather than maximum time for completion of a PhD. Although title and topic may have to be renewed after some four or five years if the thesis has not been presented, an extension of time is usually possible. It is, however, unusual for a university to permit a thesis to be submitted in less than the minimum time. Two years registered full time or three years part time is the likely stipulated minimum requirement for a PhD.

Regulations which specify a minimum time for completion exist because quality PhD research necessarily involves careful detailed teasing out and analysis of information or data. Identifying and formulating a project in the first place is usually no simple matter unless it happens to be part of the supervisor's ongoing research programme. Once data has been gathered and analysed, the final writing up stages require considerable time and frequently take longer than students expect. Conclusions, like a good wine, can be slow to mature. A thesis is likely to progress through several versions before submission. It may sometimes require unexpected additional research right at the end to exclude possible alternative interpretations of data.

Most students therefore require more than the minimum period of registration to finish their research. Full-time students usually need to be registered for at least three years. Two or three years may seem plenty of time to begin with but time, for most students, turns out to be something of a scarce commodity by the end. Although university regulations about submission are likely to allow extensions of time, the award or grant available to support a student may not be open to any such variation. So whatever period of time is available in which to complete, the PhD is worth planning systematically right from the outset.

WHAT MUST GO INTO THE TIME PLANNED?

Time is needed to identify, design and carry out the project. Then time to write it up is necessary. A PhD is first and foremost a contribution to knowledge in a subject and should afford evidence of originality through either the discovery of new facts or the exercise of independent critical power (typical criteria governing university requirements). For this to be achieved the thesis needs to be well grounded in the best research techniques and design available. A PhD student will therefore also need to devote time to research training and attendance at appropriate taught courses as well as commit time to the project itself.

Grant awarding bodies now rightly insist on this when accrediting particular departments as outlets for student research awards. A demanding taught component to the doctoral programme is increasingly the norm, the days of individual supervisor as a master craftsman and student as an apprentice are fast receding. Formulation of a personal research training plan by student and supervisor together, within the broader framework of whatever taught doctoral programme is provided, can indeed be very fruitful. Yet, whilst such recent developments in the British PhD are an obvious improvement on the past, they do nevertheless exert a greater demand for structured and disciplined use of time on the part of the student.

A PhD presents a valuable opportunity for a student to develop an awareness of research perspectives which go beyond the specific field of the thesis. Attendance at conferences, participation in the research community, imbibing the research climate in as many ways as possible, are part of this. Growth in intellectual sophistication and personal judgement are arguably both necessary conditions for, and key benefits of, undertaking a successful PhD. The price, though, is time for it all to happen.

Obtaining a PhD is an alluring but costly goal for lots of reasons. It is though all too easy to count the cost only in financial terms. The saying that 'time is money' is apt to be reversed over PhDs. Money buys time but it is the latter commodity, as well as finance, that essentially has to be planned to best advantage.

BEING CLEAR ON THE TIME COMMITMENT FROM THE OUTSET

There can be no shortcut to a PhD, only the possibility of reducing wasted time through effective planning. The essential first step in planning time is for you, the student, to be clear and realistic in making an estimate of the total time, and the time each week, that it will be necessary to set aside for your research.

Low PhD completion rates sustained by some university departments provide a cautionary tale. It can, and sometimes does, happen that after three years or so the student leaves the department with data gathering and analysis completed, first draft of the thesis written, and with a firm intention to produce the final write up as soon as possible. They then find the further time now required is overtaken by the competing demands of the new job. Time for thesis writing becomes a painful subject and the thread of the research is lost. (This can happen even when the new job is in a university academic department.) The road to hell may, it is said, be 'paved with good intentions'. Sometimes the thesis hangs on for several years or even, despite all the effort so far, is never submitted. Detailed survey evidence relating to completion rates and times for completion can be found in an article by Dunkerley and Weeks (1994).

If troubled completion scenarios are to be avoided and successful completion of the PhD within the allotted time achieved, a number of issues need to be addressed before beginning the PhD. Some of these relate to your own personal life and will be discussed more fully below. Others involve discovering key information (especially about supervision) from departments where you might try to register. For a start you might consider the following:

- What will be the reliable frequency of meeting supervisors? Is there any contract about this?
- Of what duration will supervisions be?
- How much time for the training programme is expected from the student?

It is also worth finding out how long recent students have in practice taken to complete their PhDs and, indeed, what the completion rate is.

Direct requests for information as well as scanning of information in booklets relating to the department are both appropriate and necessary. There may also be important clues to be discovered from quality assurance reports written by departments or programme evaluations written by current PhD students. In a few cases there may exist a code of practice agreed with the student union. One of the best ways of finding out about availability of supervisors and time given for supervision may quite simply be to try to meet a number of current PhD students in the department and get the insiders' view.

University departments differ in the effectiveness of their provision for PhD students. They devote funds to publicity to attract PhD students and have a need to secure their finances through the fees students pay. The would-be PhD students have a right to ask themselves 'How does the department in which I am proposing to register compare with other departments I might consider?' In the market-led economy climate in which universities compete today, students are often in a position to select departments rather than vice versa. The time allocated to the student for supervision and support is a very important criterion in deciding where to register for your PhD.

Finding out about the supervision time available from a department is only half the battle, however. A department or supervisor has every right to know how much time the student is realistically prepared to offer. Supervisors cannot work miracles over time if PhD students have never troubled to find out themselves what time they are prepared to put into obtaining a PhD! How does this compare with the time required in terms of the supervision and training in the proposed department? This is no simple question but is one that nevertheless requires a realistic answer. It is unfair to a supervisor for a student to set out on a PhD without first counting the cost in terms of time. The adequacy of departmental provision for supervision and training in terms of time needs to match up with the time the would-be PhD recruit is prepared to put into the project and sustain over a period of several years.

TIME PRESSURES AND THE REST OF LIFE

Research for a PhD does not take place in a vacuum. The tasks involved in gaining a PhD involve commitment and something of a struggle. It is sometimes easy to forget that there is life after the PhD. The greater risk, however, may be to forget to believe in life before PhD! It may be counterproductive in terms of imaginative processes, not to mention damaging to general future life prospects, to be so single-minded about time commitment to the research in hand that the rest of your activities and relationships go to waste. Some balance between PhD time planning and other spheres of life is essential.

Friendships, possibilities for getting married, upholding the quality of your family life if you are already married, time for healthy sporting pursuits, rest and leisure, are among a rather long list of very important things which will need to be taken into account in any realistic appraisal of the time needed to achieve a PhD. Not all these opportunities in your life will continue to be there for ever. The age at which the opportunity to undertake a PhD arises is clearly relevant here. The particular pattern of commitments will be different for students of different age groups. The circumstances of somebody in their early twenties who has recently graduated are likely to be very different from those of a person in their mid-forties who sets about obtaining a PhD. For everyone, however, these questions are relevant:

In planning time for a PhD ask:

- Have I time to do a PhD?
- How does the time commitment required fit in with priorities and time pressures in the rest of my life?

Martyrs sacrificed upon the altar of research do not necessarily make the best investigators, but to the extent that it is necessary for a student to forgo or postpone some facet of life more generally, he or she should be clear that this is what they have decided to do and why they did so. Then there will be less likelihood of harbouring some (unconscious) sense of resentment; a resultant manifest 'tiredness' or boredom which impedes the research also becomes correspondingly less of a risk.

In so far as time conflicts lead to some compromise the best hope of reconciling the conflicting patterns lies in first recognizing they exist and then, after discussion with everyone else concerned, making realistic time plans.

THE CASE OF PART-TIME STUDENTS

Part-timers especially are well advised to take account of the time doing a PhD is likely to take up in their life and its effect on those who depend on contact with them for their own happiness. Talking with family and friends, and in some cases with your own children, can helpfully form part of planning time for a PhD. It is the reality that presents itself to others as well as your own perceived reality which needs to be carefully judged and negotiated before embarking on a PhD.

Many PhDs today are now undertaken on a part-time basis and it is essential in these circumstances that family and friends need to be engaged with the student in the time planning. Great advantage is gained for everyone if all through the PhD the student can know that those who love them (or with whom they may be in love) can in some sense count themselves as 'insiders' and not bystanders to the important activity of research.

It is perhaps most of all crucial to take this aspect of time planning seriously if those around you are very encouraging and supportive to begin with. For in their concern to support they may fail to count the cost of support. They may fail to be alive to the change in reality involved for them in their life together with you the student.

Beyond family and friends, though, there are other regions of a person's total life space which need to be considered in planning for a PhD. Clearly there can be risks to success in their job, or in outside commitments to political or church activity, for example, if a part-time (or for that matter a full-time) student fails to evaluate time commitments in these or similar spheres relative to the PhD. The pattern of time commitment within such spheres may itself require fresh planning if it is not to render completion of the PhD impossible.

One aspect of the time planning which part-time students and their families and friends especially need to be clear about is the times in the week when the student will be getting on with their research. It is not just about how much time but *when*. An example that comes to mind here is the (successful) PhD student Lesley described by Phillida Salmon (1992) who, at least in the build up to her PhD, had to recognize that it was only after the children had gone to bed, or before they woke up, that she could realistically get on with her own studies. Time set aside at other times felt too much like time stolen from mothering time.

On a note of consolation for part-time students, it is to be noted that time planning is easier than for full-time students in that part-timers are very likely to be self-funded. To that extent the time of completion is more likely to lie within their own control, free from pressures due to awards or scholarships running out of time.

FULL-TIME PhD STUDENTS

Full-time students are not necessarily exempt from many of the foregoing points. There is, however, also a contrasting experience more likely to beset some full-time students, especially those in residence away from home and family, or who come from overseas. A sense of being faced with too unstructured a daily pattern of life is common and there may arise feelings of stagnation, uselessness, low sense of personal achievement, loneliness or even anomie.

Students coming straight from completion of an undergraduate degree, with all its hassle of finals preparation, may be particularly vulnerable in the early period of PhD registration before the plan or precise research topic is settled with the supervisor. It is true the dangers are less so today than in former times when there were fewer requirements to attend taught courses as part of a PhD training, they do though still exist.

To avoid the early period in the PhD registration becoming something of an empty time, active planning of the use of time is necessary to both resolve research topic and design, and take full advantage of the period as a lull before the storm. It is a time for a student to be able to attend to issues of developing his or her research sophistication more broadly. It is a time which is precious and will not be so available once the momentum of the research project itself gets fully under way.

PLANNING PhD TIME IS A TWO WAY PROCESS

Especially in the early phases of the project, but really all through, there are two time plans which need to be synchronized. The first is a student's own planning and it is largely within your own control. The second concerns the supervisor's use of time and is mainly outside your immediate control.

What steps can a student take to make sure they have a regular slot in the supervisor's timetable – a slot they can count on and for which they can identify targets to be met? The answer will be different in different set ups but it is not a bad idea for a student to resolve from the outset never to leave one supervision without having made sure they are clear about the date and time of the next one and what the agreed action points and targets are which have to be met meantime.

In this way you will have not only a better basis for day-to-day planning of time but it may also help you feel less anxious about whether you are doing all that is necessary for successful progress. Boundaries free from ambiguity about who is responsible for what, you or your supervisor, and regular meetings within a planned time schedule, are also the best way to build a secure working relationship between supervisor and research student.

TIME AND MOTIVATION TO COMPLETE A PhD

In one sense time is a finite objectively measurable commodity. In another sense it is better thought of as subjective. Time working on a PhD can have a very different feel about it depending upon whether a student has chosen a topic of genuine and continuing interest to him or her or whether somehow he or she has had a topic foisted upon them. Time is therefore needed in the beginning for exploring the possibilities within several topic areas rather than snatching at the first feasible topic which presents itself.

This may pose something of a dilemma for part-time students. They may wonder whether or not to choose a PhD topic which is in some way directly related to the life they lead and work they do. Time economies and convenience are likely if your research is in some sense continuous with either your daily occupation or leisure interests.

A teacher who had recently successfully obtained a PhD in educational psychology put it to me this way:

> I found it important to ask myself 'Can this topic be integrated so that it adds to rather than detracts from what I do at school . . . so that I never feel I'm taking away from what is important; that it's never an intrusive task?' I needed to avoid a 'bolt on' feeling or any sense of add on skills.

She went on to say that unless there had been some such sense of 'seamless' continuity she would never have been able to keep going through the inevitable administrative and organizational frustrations that can arise in a PhD when she had to make arrangements for experimental subjects to be available etc.

Not everyone would take this view, however. A university teacher, still engaged in the final stages of write up, complained that the closeness of her research topic to her academic teaching was a drawback:

> It's all too much like what I'm doing anyway . . . I have to give myself short term rewards as coping aids . . . it's all about coping with yourself.

For conscientious university or school teachers who are also engaged in their in their own PhD research, as well as for many other part-time PhD students working in occupations where the progress and well-being of others much depends upon them, the conflicts of loyalty between spending time promoting their study and the needs of their own students can be very severe.

TIME MANAGEMENT AND THE PHASES OF RESEARCH: SOME PRACTICAL STEPS

Since working for a PhD is not like painting by numbers, it has to be admitted that time planning cannot finally be reduced to a formula. Some degree of unpredictability is sure to exist. Nevertheless, forward planning is of obvious major importance if a PhD is to be completed within the time covered by the research award or the time you have set yourself as a part-time student. It is possible to identify phases through which the empirical research must pass before attaining its final thesis form. In an empirical study these might be as follows:

1 Becoming familiar with the resources and courses available to help you at the institution where you are studying.
2 Identifying and formulating your project precisely and clearly in terms of purposes, issues and questions to be addressed.
3 Identifying through bibliographic search and other means material for review chapters (including methodological reviews) and writing these chapters. In some cases this will lead to statement of formal hypotheses.
4 Deciding upon research design and designing research instruments for the study. This will include arranging and carrying out pre-pilot and pilot work for the main part of your study.
5 Making arrangements to access the sample in the main study and, in advance, arranging for facilities to record and analyse data.
6 Execution of main study.
7 Data analysis.
8 Interpretation of data.
9 Final write up of thesis.
10 Getting thesis into final presentation form and bound.

The phases listed are only intended as notional guides and just what is entailed in each is part of the substance of other chapters in the book. Furthermore the step-by-step progress is not so absolute in all cases as is perhaps suggested. In that sense they are phases rather than strict stages.

The point made is that although there will be differences according to opportunity, circumstance and the nature of any given individual research project, a project development plan can be made in a precise way which charts the phases according to a timescale.

Points to reckon with:

- Identifying target dates for completion of each phase is important. So too are possible sub-phases within each main phase. What will need to have been achieved or put in place before the next phase can begin?
- Considered on a monthly timescale, what will have to have been achieved by the end of each month, what are the monthly targets?
- The plan will need to set out phases of the project in a tidy sequential order. Make allowance for the fact that some of the phases can run in parallel when you draw up your timescale (e.g. review of existing literature can profitably overlap with formulating initial research questions and hypotheses, or even a pilot phase of the research).
- The write-up phase at the end is usually an unexpectedly lengthy process, even if much of the writing up has usefully been done as you have gone along. Allow plenty of time for second and even third drafts. What can be written up in a fairly final form earlier in the time plan whilst the data gathering and analysis is in progress?
- Suppose you fall behind with the targets – what safety time can be built into your plan to allow for catch-up periods? If you do fall behind, at least you will know by just how much you do need to catch up!

Ambitious though it may sound, it can be helpful to start with the date you intend to finish the thesis and work the phases backwards in time up to the present. Within that you can adjust times in order to finalize a critical path to your goal of PhD.

It is essential that the researcher be in charge of the plan and not the plan in charge of the researcher. The plan is there to help, not to enslave. Rescheduling and modification are open to the researcher and may become necessary as the project evolves or as unforseen difficulties or new opportunities arise. Even if you fall behind your time schedule for the PhD it is better to know that this is so and having a plan will help you recognize that you have fallen behind. You can replan accordingly. If things are going according to schedule your plan will help you know this too and you can, perhaps, enjoy the fact of your progress.

It may all seem rather tedious to plan time in a detailed way but it is worth doing so. It needs a conscious resolve and effort to take the trouble to devise such a plan and it requires the plan to be set down in written form with target dates stated. In some cases a week by week time planner such as is available from many stationers may be helpful, but other kinds of time chart are also possible. Phillips and Pugh (1994) provide a time-line diagram which you may find helpful as an example of a time-based programme of work. Their chapter discussing the PhD process, both in its psychological aspects and in its more practical aspects of timetabling and time management, is a good one to refer to for further reading.

THE VALUE OF DEADLINES

In the same chapter Phillips and Pugh emphasize the importance of deadlines. They point out that deadlines do not just have the obvious power to motivate the student. For the supervisor they provide a potential basis on which to monitor the development of the student's thinking and growth in autonomous skill within their topic area, as well as for ascertaining that an agreed amount of reading, written or practical work has been completed. Where the supervisor (sometimes out of well-intentioned but misplaced concern that they may be pressurizing the student too much and causing stress) is not in the habit of setting deadlines, the student, it is suggested, should create 'pseudo-deadlines' for themselves and tell their supervisors.

When deadlines are not being met it is important for both the student and the supervisor to work out just what the difficulty is and find ways to remove obstacles, practical or personal, to progress so that time can be saved, as well as frustration, and embarrassment relieved. This is part of the value of having deadlines. It can be hard, though, if it is left to the student to initiate discussion of difficulties they are encountering in meeting deadlines. It can be even harder to initiate this discussion if it is the supervisor who has not met deadlines in commenting on the student's submitted work, or has failed to keep appointments, etc. It is worthwhile for the student to face up to the issues even here, however, and given a tactful approach it may result also in a more open relationship with your supervisor in the future.

THE IMPORTANCE OF MILESTONES ALONG THE ROAD TO A PhD

Making a clear-cut plan has the advantage that it can create the time for you to enjoy the important parts of the rest of your life outside research without undue anxiety. By setting milestones along the road, ambiguity about making measured and satisfactory progress can be relieved.

This may help conquer the common feeling many researchers experience that the research is getting too much to carry on with, there are too many diffuse strands to cope with and the end will never be in sight. Setting clear, short-term priority goals which are credible, achievable, within your control and the attainment of which will be visible to yourself and others, is important.

One important milestone you may wish to include in your plan is the target date by which you hope to achieve the upgrade from MPhil to PhD. If the department in which you are registered is one where this is no formality, its use as a progress indicator is very helpful (see Chapter 5 on this). What other such progress indicators as milestones can you suggest for yourself?

By achieving progress according to milestones along the way, you can have a feeling of success and achievement as you go along rather than it all hanging upon the final submission of the thesis. It is fair and humane to yourself to need sometimes to know you are successful and not just a struggler along the line!

'URGENT' AND 'IMPORTANT'

Sometimes keeping in mind a simple distinction between what is *urgent* and what is *important* may help you sort the difficulty of time management. Top priority should go to things which are both important and urgent, next should come matters which are important but not necessarily urgent, third come those things which are urgent but not important, and finally most obviously lowest priority belongs to matters which are neither important nor urgent. The temptation is to give priority to something that is urgent or perhaps routine and easy to achieve at the moment, but in itself of no great importance, at the expense of something less pressing at the moment but of great long-term importance. Putting off the important but not immediately urgent things may lead to time pressures later where time-urgency is no basis for tackling difficult research.

WHAT ARE THE LIKELY SOURCES OF HOLD UP AND DELAY IN A PhD? HOW CAN TIME PLANNING HELP?

As already mentioned, finding a topic that you feel you want to research and feel comfortable with may take longer than you imagine. The first year of a project may in some cases be clouded with uncertainty in this way and this can be truly de-motivating. As a guideline Gottlieb (1994) suggests that after six months or so a student should at least be able to 'encapsulate in one long sentence the central question which the research addresses'.

In writing the chapters of a thesis which review previous research, there may sometimes be considerable delays in gaining access to the books, documents and journals that need to be read. Making time for forward planning can be helpful here. Once available they often take much longer to work through than expected, especially if too many notes are being taken or no systematic way of recording summary points has been put in place.

Even once formulated the topic may take an unexpected or elusive twist, or, in the human sciences, difficulties to do with the availability of respondents or experimental subjects may occur. More hold ups to be endured! In educational research, for example, delays whilst waiting for parental or governors' permission to work with pupils, not to mention the sudden realization that the school holidays are upon you and your subjects will disappear for a while, all have the potential to upset even well-laid plans.

Once data is gathered in, quantitative data analysis can, of course, be much speedier than in the past because of the everyday use of computers. True, but don't bank on it too much! It can take weeks to enter the data on the computer and furthermore there may be all sorts of difficulties which take time to resolve in deciding which analyses you are going to attempt, which statistics you propose to use and whether and how much time to invest in preliminary simple number counts, etc., in order to get to know your data better and to discern its shape in a descriptive or exploratory manner.

The temptation here is to enter just everything and to instruct the computer to get on with every statistical test you can think of. Thoughtless and ill-disciplined approaches of this kind can indeed be a false time economy. It is not just that the time required to enter all the data may be greatly increased; it is also likely that you will be swamped by the computer output. It may take days, even weeks to wade through it all just to arrive at the main points on which to concentrate for presentation in the thesis.

Some compromise is therefore necessary in planning time for data analysis which keeps a balance between giving you as researcher the chance to learn its main contours and outlines whilst at the same time keeping whatever models or hypotheses you have generated firmly in sight.

When it comes to analysing qualitative data there may be long delays while you read it all through and, if you do decide to enter it in some content analysis program on the computer, delays can sometimes occur while you learn the complexities of the program or of your own coding scheme. It may lead to an economy of time in the end and allow all sorts of analyses to proceed but the time required en route can be a boring hard grind. It is therefore easy to underestimate how long it will take.

Once the data is analysed and under control timewise, as it were, there may be further delays at the discussion and interpretation stage of write up. Supervisors are apt to start going through the thesis in a very detailed and argumentative way and this can feel like unnecessary delay, especially if you think you know what you have discovered. Sometimes, too, they take overlong, as it may seem to the student, to read submitted chapters. This is precisely because what they are being asked to do requires careful detailed work on their part and considerable time investment within a world of other commitments. PhD students are apt to become very impatient at this point and to believe that the supervisor is being unnecessarily pedantic. It all may seem too long and drawn out.

The final straw is when no time has been planned at the end for chasing up bibliographic details. This can really cause delay and frustration. Some time allowed for this is essential, though the obvious answer is to make sure that some time is invested in keeping adequate reference details as you go along.

Time planning cannot eradicate all of the frustrations, twists and delays in producing a thesis. To be forewarned is, however, to be forearmed. Simply recognizing the normality of it all helps save time as it reduces frustration.

Thinking ahead and making time plans which, though they specify dates for achieving certain goals in a realistic way, also make allowance for delay and envisage reformulation if necessary, is another way of easing the difficulties. All through it is always better to travel with some timetable in mind, albeit a revised one, rather than to travel merely hopefully or angrily because of unanticipated delay. Planning so that you always have something else you can be getting on with if you get stuck or delayed also helps.

WHEN IT ALL BECOMES TOO MUCH!

Careful previous contingency planning of time may not have been sufficient to anticipate the problems. The volume of work needed suddenly seems overwhelming, deadlines are too pressing, there are too many unfinished tasks on hand and too many uncertainties which all require to be resolved at once. Days of routine in the library are replaced by a demand for intense unremitting action. Worse still, much of what needs to be done and the problems awaiting to be overcome may lie beyond your control. For reasons such as these, academic research can become a highly pressurizing activity. If it goes on for too long, emotional exhaustion, a low sense of personal accomplishment, a feeling that life is going nowhere, even feeling less of a whole person, can result.

There is no infallible remedy for such stress. Being aware of its nature and that to some degree it is 'normal' helps a bit, trying to take whatever steps are possible to regain control of the situation is important, and being prepared to cope with your own fears and panics by recognizing them for what they are and seeking to come to terms with them, even distancing them to an extent, may help you live through the problems. Certainly having some previous frame-work of time planning which you can now begin to revise is better than no previous plan. The one thing not to do is to suffer in silence. It is a mistake to keep quiet about how you feel or deny your feelings.

Discuss your time pressures with your supervisor, talk with other research students, get suggestions from whatever other support network you have. If time pressures begin to be too much, admit it and seek help from an academic counsellor or the student health centre or whatever similar resource is available.

POSTSCRIPT ON INDIVIDUAL DIFFERENCES

There are some wise words of caution to be found in the writing of Phillida Salmon referred to earlier (Salmon 1992). She would be unlikely to go along with the rather firm and specific advice about targets, deadlines, built-in order of tasks, time plans formulated in advance to drive the PhD project along, which have been advocated in the present chapter.

> There can be no universally viable timetable, no generalizable order of work, no uniform number of hours per day, no standard mechanism for engaging or disengaging with the project. Everyone has to find within themselves ways of working on their own piece of research which both fit with the rest of their lives and – at least at times – bring about a sense of progress. All this is very difficult. The creative process is itself notoriously capricious.
>
> (Salmon 1992: 22)

The role of the supervisor here is one of responsiveness and of being alive to the student's underlying sense of commitment, especially when he or she may himself or herself have lost sight of this.

The point is well made and is backed up by sensitive discussion and justification, not least by illustration drawn from the ten PhD students described by Salmon. It may well be, though, only part of the story. What is needed for PhD students to succeed may properly be something along the lines set out in this chapter but tempered by recognition of the individuality of each research student, their temperament, their circumstances and the nature of their project.

Certainly in all time planning one thing which needs to taken into account is the fact that different individuals have different ways of working, different tolerances of time pressure and require different degrees of urgency to produce their optimal best performance. Time deadlines therefore have a varied significance for different individuals. This needs to be kept in mind and may be of some importance if you, for example, compare your own rate of progress with that of others in their PhD research. Likewise it needs to be kept in mind if you seek advice from other students on your own progress.

It is doubtful, however, whether saying to yourself that you are a person who can only work as deadlines approach is ever a good thing to do. Likewise hearing from others that they can only work with deadlines in mind is not necessarily the best way for you. Allow for your own way of working in making your time plans by all means, but do not fall into the trap of letting such talk be an excuse for not formulating well-worked time schedules. For these can play an important part in making sure you finally arrive at PhD graduation day not just as a successful candidate but also in a reasonably composed frame of mind!

REFERENCES

Dunkerley, D. and Weeks, J. (1994) 'Social Science Research Degrees: Completion Times and Rates', in Burgess, R.G. (ed.) *Postgraduate Education and Training in the Social Sciences*, London: Jessica Kingsley.

Fisher, S. (1994) *Stress in Academic Life: The Mental Assembly Line*, Buckingham: Society for Research into Higher Education and Open University.

Gottlieb, N. (1994) 'Supervising the Writing of a Thesis', in Zuber-Skerritt, O. and Ryan, Y. (eds) *Quality in Postgraduate Education*, London: Kogan Page.

Phillips, E.M. and Pugh, D.S. (1994) *How to Get a PhD*, Buckingham: Open University Press.

Salmon, P. (1992) *Achieving a PhD – Ten Students' Experience*, Stoke-on-Trent: Trentham.

Chapter 5

Problems of supervision

Norman Graves

INTRODUCTION

Supervision presents problems for both the student and the supervisor. I can recall my own feelings as a student when supervision was unstructured and limited in extent. I was unsure as to what I and my fellow students could expect in the way of guidance. Similarly, when I began supervising students many years later, whilst I was clear I wanted to give as much help as possible, I was also unsure as to how far I should insist on students coming to see me regularly, or allow them to come and see me when they felt they needed some help. There were then no guidelines for students and staff and much depended on what the supervisor was able and willing to do, or on the persistence of students in badgering their supervisors. Today things have changed for the better, but problems still remain and these will be discussed in this chapter.

Let me outline the nature of these problems. They occur at certain critical points in the process of supervision. First, there is the question of who the supervisor should be. Second, how may one develop a fruitful relationship with one's supervisor and how may this relationship change over time, as the different stages of the research process evolve. Third, there is the need to establish just what the limits to a supervisor's function are if the research to be undertaken is genuinely the student's and not the supervisor's. Lastly there is the role of the supervisor in relation to the examination process.

Essentially the supervision of a thesis involves a negotiated progression, during which the tutor initiates the student into the techniques of academic research; the student on his part becomes socialized into the academic community and gradually adopts the mores of that community whilst maintaining sufficient independence of thought to make possible the creative enterprise that true research entails.

STUDENTS CHOOSING A SUPERVISOR

Students embarking on a three or more year stint of research work vary considerably in their initial approach to the task. Some have a clear idea of what they want to do, and know where the expertise in the field of their choice is to be found. Presumably such students will seek to be registered in the institution where the experts in the area concerned work; they may then discuss their proposals with one or two experts and then ask one of them to supervise their research. From experience I suspect that such students are in a minority in the humanities and social sciences. Many have but a vague notion of what they wish to research and whilst they may be aware of the names of some experts in their general field of study, this may be insufficiently detailed to enable them to pinpoint an individual or group of specialists who might be useful as supervisors. They may also lack the confidence to approach such persons even if they know of their existence.

Thus the first task when proposing to undertake research is to narrow down the area in which one is proposing to work and locate the expertise in the field. This may be fairly obvious in some areas from the journal articles one has read, particularly those that report research and its findings. For example in the area of European studies a student might be particularly interested in regional economic development in Italy and find that the name of Russell King occurred frequently in articles on this topic. Similarly if the field to be researched is nineteenth-century educational history, the name of Richard Aldrich may be found cropping up in books and journals concerned with this subject. Usually the publications concerned indicate the institution in which the person works, so that it is fairly easy to track him or her down. If you as a potential research student are particularly keen to work with a particular supervisor, there is no harm in writing to him or her and outlining what you propose to do and asking the person concerned whether he or she would be willing to take you on. Of course there is no guarantee that your wishes will be acceded to, since procedures in the institution may not allow a potential tutor to take such a decision alone, or the tutor concerned may already be overloaded with students.

Such a straightforward approach to choosing a supervisor may not be available. You may well be a mature student undertaking research on a part-time basis and only one university is within easy reach. You may be the holder of a grant which is tied in to a particular centre. In such cases, which I suspect are the majority, then you will need to conform to the procedures of the institution to which you are applying. Nevertheless, getting early information about the relevant members of staff of that institution will repay the time taken to make enquiries. Where can such information be obtained? Many colleges, institutes or even departments publish lists of the research and teaching interests of their staff. To this may be added an annual register of staff publications. The latter is often a better guide to recent research undertaken by staff since the stated interests of university teachers are often rather wider than their research expertise. It is important to distinguish among the publications those that report on substantive research projects and those which, though they may be raising important issues, are not strictly concerned with research. By such enquiries you may be able to identify someone who might be an appropriate supervisor (ESRC 1984: 6). If you think this is the person you may wish to work with, then write to him or her and ask for an appointment. You may get this person interested in your proposal or s/he may be able to indicate someone else who might be a more appropriate supervisor.

The procedure when applying to the institution of your choice will be something like the following. The prospectus of the institution concerned will indicate that application forms may be obtained from the Registrar, or the Head of the Graduate School, the Student Programmes Office, or some similar title. These forms vary in style and content according to the institution one is applying to, but all will require, apart from the usual personal information, some indication of the kind of research the student wants to embark upon. It is in your interest to be as precise as possible about this, indicating, if relevant, any previous work you have done in this area, plus any work of yours which has been published. If you have had prior discussions about your proposal with a member of a particular department, state this on your form, as the person receiving your form may not know this. This will enable the person dealing with your application to direct it to the department or member of staff whose research interest is nearest to yours. It does not matter if you are not completely sure of the direction your proposed research will take, as subsequent discussion with the member of staff will help you to clarify this issue.

It could well turn out that only one person has expertise in the area you propose to investigate, in which case there may be little choice as to who your supervisor will be. Sometimes, no one is an expert in this area and the head of the department will have to ask someone whose interests are nearest to yours. This may not be a great disadvantage, granted the person chosen has sufficient knowledge of the appropriate research methods. One factor which may affect the choice of supervisor is the number of research students a particular member of staff has 'collected'. I knew of one case where someone was responsible for well over twenty students. It seemed clear that such a person could not possibly give the kind of attention required to all those students. Hence many part-time students were, so to speak, sleeping partners and their research languished. Most institutions now have a norm of not more than six research students per member of staff, and in many cases the actual number of students per staff member is much lower. It may, however, be useful to make discreet enquiries as to how many research students a potential supervisor is currently responsible for and what proportion of his or her students complete within three or four years. One needs to bear in mind in present circumstances the fact that the growth in the number of students in higher education has not been matched by a growth in the number of staff owing to financial restrictions on university funding. Consequently the increase in the staff/student ratio is inevitable (Fig. 5.1).

Over and above the question of overall financing, one needs to be aware that the financing of research in each institution depends on the Research Assessment Exercise (RAE). This tends to favour (however unfair this may seem) those institutions whose research output is already high, that is the older universities. Hence if you want to work in an institution with a vibrant research culture, with a supervisor currently active in research, your choice is again limited, through no fault of the newer universities (AUT-NATFHE 1993:10).

FORMAL PROCEDURES FOR APPOINTING A SUPERVISOR

In many institutions the registrar will send an application to a relevant department which will probably have a Departmental

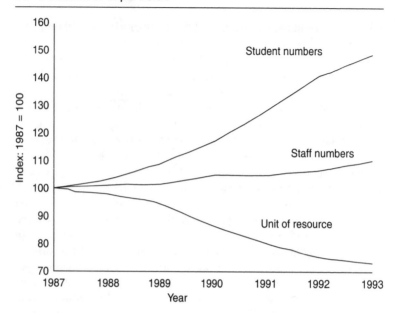

Figure 5.1 Staff numbers vs student numbers vs unit of resource
Source: AUT/NATFHE Confederation 1993

Research Committee. Occasionally a student may require two supervisors. This is the case when, for example, a student's research area involves both knowledge of the subject area of the research and knowledge of computing to deal with data gathered in the process of research. This may happen in many fields, though today many supervisors in particular subject areas also have computing expertise.

In education, it often happens that research in pupils' understanding of subject matter in, for example, the natural sciences, benefits from the inputs of both a specialist in science education and a psychologist. Whilst joint supervision seems reasonable in these circumstances, it does create on occasion problems for the student, who finds that s/he has to interact with two people who may not always see eye to eye on a particular issue (Burgess *et al*. 1994: 24). It is probably best in cases of joint supervision if one supervisor is nominated as the principal supervisor, and the other is seen as an additional advisor dealing with technical matters on which the student requires advice. I have found that this system tends to work well, though occasionally advisors on computing are sometimes understandably irate at having to deal with problems which need not have arisen had they been consulted earlier. It is therefore important for the principal supervisor to keep his or her colleague informed of all decisions taken with respect to the student's research and to consult him/her on issues which arise.

To return to the formal procedures, the registrar's office will be responsible for checking that the applicant has the necessary prior qualifications. Granted all is well the Departmental Research Committee will normally arrange to interview the candidate and will subsequently discuss who should supervise the student. Usually allocation will be to the tutor with the appropriate expertise and interest. Clearly, if a tutor has already discussed the research proposal with the prospective student, this will come out at the Departmental Research Committee meeting, and usually, unless there is a major obstacle, and if the tutor wants to take on the student, the Committee will decide accordingly. All such decisions will be reported to the registrar so that a record may be kept centrally as to which tutor is responsible for that student. In many institutions it is usual to register a student initially for an MPhil degree (i.e. a master's research degree rather than a doctorate) and to await a positive report on his/her progress at the end of the first year's work before upgrading the registration to PhD. Such a decision is often taken by the Departmental Research Committee. It is important that the student is made aware that such upgrading is not an automatic process, and that even if upgrading occurs, at the examination, an MPhil may be awarded if the work is judged worthy of an award but of an insufficient calibre to be awarded a PhD.

DEVELOPING A FRUITFUL RELATIONSHIP WITH A SUPERVISOR

As in all partnerships, this is a two-way process. Both student and supervisor must wish the relationship to succeed. This makes it sound as though we are dealing with a failing marriage; in most cases this is far from the truth, but the pressures on both tutor and student are such that problems may arise. Let me state unequivocally that the primary responsibility lies with the supervisor, though this does not prevent the student from taking the initiative when s/he deems it necessary.

For example, it will be the tutor's responsibility to:

- develop with the student a plan for the research, including the need to carry out a literature search around the proposed topic;
- make sure the student is aware of the research training available and to suggest what training courses s/he should attend (the institution should have a booklet outlining what courses are available) (Student Programmes Office 1995a);
- tease out precisely what the research is trying to discover;
- discuss the nature and sources of the data to be collected;
- suggest possible methods of analysis;
- discuss the interpretation of the results.

In the early stages, the student will often feel unsure and should be encouraged to pose questions, even such simple questions as to how to carry out the literature search and how to record the findings. At that stage the student should not be allowed to feel that s/he has been abandoned to his/her own devices and regular weekly meetings should be held to monitor progress, deal with problems as they arise and review the research plan in the light of what has been found out.

One problem area is that of the research training courses. Many students, particularly part-time students, are reluctant to attend these. There are two basic reasons: first students often argue that many are minimally relevant to what their research is about; second and re-inforced by the first reason, they plead a shortage of time. Whilst there is some truth in these reasons, the supervisor should not be unduly influenced by such pleading. From a purely practical point of view students financed by such bodies as the Economic and Social Research Council (ESRC) are bound by the terms of their grant to follow research training courses. The research councils see the purpose of their financing PhD students as a means of training new researchers with knowledge of a broad range of research methods. Further, although some aspects of research training courses may not be directly relevant to a student's immediate concerns, the insight they get into a variety of research methods makes them aware of techniques used by research reports that they may use in their own literature search. These may also suggest to them methods which they had originally not considered using. In any event, courses are often so organized that they are often run at two levels: level 1 at which the students learns what the research methods purport to do; and level 2 which the student only needs to follow if s/he intends using that particular technique in her/his own research. Perhaps the greatest resistance to research training courses, in the humanities and social sciences, comes from those who have a fear of quantitative techniques. Many students imagine that qualitative and quantitative techniques are alternative rather than complementary methods. Thus the supervisor may need to be very persuasive to get the student to follow these courses, though now most institutions often make attendance at such courses compulsory for research students.

In the course of time the student will become more confident and, as the research develops, weekly meetings with the supervisor may not be necessary. Such a recommendation applies to full-time students (SERC 1983: 9); it needs to be modified for part-time students who will probably not make enough progress in one week to make a weekly meeting useful. My own experience as a part-time student would tend to confirm this, since the exigencies of one's professional life may mean that in some weeks very little research work will be accomplished. However, as Derek May indicates in Chapter 4, there is a need to maintain a balance between the desire to move the research forward and the demands of one's working and family life.

The student needs feedback. There is nothing more disheartening than to be working hard at one's research and not to know whether one is making satisfactory progress nor be sure whether the standard of the work produced is appropriate for the standard of a PhD. Now clearly, in the early stages it will be difficult to make any judgement about standards, but it will be possible for the supervisor to indicate whether the research is gathering the sort of evidence required in the light of the aims of the research, and whether the amount produced is reasonable in the time available. Later, the student may be asked to write up the findings of the literature survey. Writing initial chapters will prove a useful exercise, since it will enable the student to sift out from the totality of what s/he has gathered that which is strictly relevant to the problem being tackled. Here the supervisor will be able to make an initial judgement about how far the student is able to marshall ideas and select the relevant from what may be interesting but marginal to the thesis. By going over what has been written, s/he may counsel the student about the clarity and economy of her/his writing and make valuable suggestions for future written work (Young et al. 1987: 59–60). Excellent guidance on writing a thesis is given by James Hartley in Chapter 6.

By this time the student will be approaching the end of the first year. In some institutions the student and supervisor will be required to complete a report form which may have a format similar

---

RESEARCH STUDENT'S ANNUAL REPORT

Name: Department:

- - - - - - - - - - - - - - - - - - -

Supervisor: Year

- - - - - - - - - - - - - - - - - - -

MPhil/PhD Subject area:

- - - - - - - - - - - - - - - - - - -

Title and brief details of research:

- - - - - - - - - - - - - - - - - - -

WORK DONE DURING YEAR

1   Research training undertaken

2   Main research questions tackled

3   Progress made to date

4   Number of meetings with supervisor:

Autumn term

Spring term

Summer term

5   Plan for next academic year

6   Estimated date of completion

- - - - - - - - - - - - - - - - - - -

SUPERVISOR'S COMMENTS

(In cases of joint supervision, the principal supervisor should, after completion, send on the form to the second supervisor)

- - - - - - - - - - - - - - - - - - -

Signature(s) of supervisors   Date:

Form to be sent to the chair of the Dept Research Committee and a copy to the student.

Figure 5.2 Research student's annual report

to Figure 5.2. Such a report will enable the Departmental Research Committee (or some similar body) to assess the student's progress and make any necessary recommendations. Any feedback which the student gets from people other than the supervisor is often welcomed by the student. In the course of my career, I have often been approached by research students in my own department who were supervised by colleagues but who wanted to discuss matters with someone else. They did so not because they did not trust their own supervisors, but because they wanted to hear another viewpoint on an issue. Similarly some of my own students approached colleagues of mine about their work. This happened more often with full-time students than with part-time students, the latter being short of time and colleagues being less easily available in the evening.

Another source of feedback is that given by other research students. The Departmental Research Committee should normally arrange a series of research seminars so that students may be aware of what other students are doing, the methods they are using, the problems they have met and how they have (or have not) tackled them. Occasionally, it is useful to arrange for institution-wide seminars in which students from different departments meet and find out what research is going on in other departments. Some cross-fertilization of ideas goes on as a result of such seminars. Students who are at an early stage of their work should be asked to outline their research proposals to such seminars. Students who are more advanced in their work can often make very helpful suggestions about procedures, sources and methods of data analysis.

Granted all has gone reasonably well in the first year, the relationship with the supervisor should develop along fruitful lines. The supervisor will begin to feel that the student can be trusted to develop her/his work along more independent lines. The student will be more confident, s/he will be spending much time gathering data, either in the field or from documentary sources. Which data and how much will probably have been discussed at an earlier stage, but when the student feels that s/he has enough material to begin analysing it, the tutor should probably be asked to comment on whether the quantity and quality of the information gathered is adequate. Students, especially those with a perfectionist tendency, are often afraid that they may not have enough material. In most cases the supervisor may be able to reassure them. However, should a question arise about the adequacy of the data, then it is far better that this is spotted then than at the examination stage.

UPGRADING FROM MPhil TO PhD

It is at this stage that students who have initially registered for an MPhil will consider asking to have their registration upgraded to PhD. Whilst practice varies from institution to institution, in general students will be asked to submit a request (often on a special form) to the Departmental Research Committee, indicating;

- What research training they have undergone
- How that training relates to the research they are undertaking
- The detailed plan of their research
- What writing they have already produced
- How the proposed research will meet the university's criteria for a successful PhD (Student Programmes Office 1995b)

This last point is a difficult one for the student. Universities usually state that a PhD thesis is one which shows that a distinct contribution to knowledge has been made, that there is evidence of originality by the discovery of new facts and/or the exercise of critical judgement and that the thesis must have a full bibliography and references. Inevitably at an early stage, the student may be hard put to indicate exactly how his or her work can be shown to be original; s/he can only make an inspired guess as to the sort of thing which will be discovered. In this matter the supervisor can be helpful by indicating an appropriate form of words. However, the tutor cannot prejudge something that rightly it is the duty of a committee to judge. There are cases where the decision is not a difficult one; the research questions posed are very interesting, the method of tackling them sound and the amount of data either gathered or in the process of being gathered is sufficient for the student to bring the project to a successful conclusion. Doubtful cases are usually those where there is a question mark as to whether the student has posed a problem of sufficient depth to warrant research at PhD level; the level of sophistication of the analysis may be low; the skill in handling historical data may be of doubtful quality and the extent of critical judgement limited. Strictly, the supervisor should have warned him or her about this in the early stages of the research, but sometimes the supervisor may not be aware of just how much evidence may be available. I once had a case of an overseas student who proposed to gather his data in his native country. It sounded a very reasonable proposition, but when he returned to his country he found that the amount of evidence he could gather was much less than he had expected. As a result it proved impossible to upgrade him, though later he chose another topic for a PhD.

In cases where there is disagreement as to whether the student should be upgraded, the institution should have procedures in place enabling the matter to be resolved by arbitration. Usually the dean of research or some such person will be involved.

THE SUPERVISOR IN THE LATER STAGES OF THE RESEARCH

Assuming all has gone well and the student is now well on his or her way to the analysis and interpretation of the data, there will be less need for regular meetings with the supervisor. Indeed if students are literally out 'in the field', in Paris or Chamonix gathering data in, for example, La Bibliothèque Nationale or on an Alpine glacier, then meetings with tutors will be well nigh impossible (Becher *et al.* 1994). But if the student is available, then s/he should ask to see the tutor to report on progress and to discuss any problem that has arisen. Indeed one could argue that in these later stages when the student can see the research beginning to take shape, then only s/he can know when it is necessary to approach the supervisor. On the other hand, if a supervisor finds that there has been no contact with the student for some time, then alarm bells should start ringing; something may be wrong. In such a case the tutor should ask to see the student to sort things out. The problem may concern the research directly, but often it is a personal or financial problem. As Patrick O'Brien states 'a difficult but important part of the job is to insure that the unavoidable pangs of self doubt and sense of isolation experienced by large numbers of students do not become insuperable obstacles to completing a dissertation'; and a little later he adds 'Supervision involves a quotient of therapy' (O'Brien 1995). Of course some problems may have to be referred to the welfare officer or the student counselling service, but a little sympathetic understanding by the supervisor will often go a long way to solving the problem. This is particularly true of overseas students who may have cause to feel even more isolated than home students (Aspland and O'Donoghue 1994).

I came across one problem when reading a chapter of a student's draft thesis. As the reading progressed, I suddenly became aware that the style of writing had changed, and this new style went on for about three pages before reverting to the previous style. I at once suspected plagiarism. Given the subject of the thesis and my knowledge of the field, I knew it did not come from a published work, so I located a thesis in the library in this area and sure enough the passage had been extracted from a thesis which had been presented two years before. I confronted the student with the evidence, and this proved a salutary lesson.

As the student begins to write the thesis, a question often arises as to how far the supervisor should be involved. After all it is the student's work which will be examined, not the supervisor's. This is true, but the supervisor can help the student by commenting on the clarity of his or her exposition, suggesting the elimination of irrelevant material (or padding) and by pointing out how far the inferences made from the data collected are logically acceptable. The final decision as to what goes in the thesis must be the student's, as s/he is the owner of the work and has to take ultimate responsibility for it. Thus though a tutor may well say to a student 'I would not present the thesis in its present form, if I were you', the student should still be free to present it if s/he is so minded. I recognize, however, that the boot may be on the other foot. When completion rates are an issue, the tutor may well suggest that a thesis might be presented to boost the department's performance indicator, when the student may feel uncertain. In either event, the student should be the ultimate arbiter of when the thesis is ready for examination.

COMMUNICATION BREAKDOWN

Estelle Phillips devotes a whole chapter to this topic in a recent book (Phillips 1994a: 134–141), and avers that 'communications breakdown is rampant amongst students and their supervisors'. Whilst my own experience would suggest that this is perhaps exaggerated, it is useful to take note of what she says since this is based on research over a fifteen-year period in which students and their supervisors were interviewed separately. Broadly by 'communications breakdown', Phillips means those situations in which the perceptions of student and supervisors as to what is happening are at odds. The student may be quite satisfied with the supervision s/he is getting, whereas the supervisor may think the student requires too much guidance and will not in the end become an autonomous researcher. A variant on such a case is where the student believes s/he is being too closely supervised, but the supervisor thinks that only the formal meetings count as supervisions and not the casual enquiries as to how the student is getting on. At the other extreme, the supervisor may believe the student is getting on fine and does not want to interfere too much, whereas the student believes s/he is not being given much help. There are all sorts of combinations of differing attitudes between students and supervisors which lead to misunderstandings, not many of which are fatal for the student in achieving his or her PhD, but which lead to the research process being less efficient and less agreeable than it might otherwise be.

All of these problems result from a lack of openness between the student and his or her supervisor. Diffidence is one of the elements in such a situation and this may play an important role in the case of overseas students. I well remember an able student from an Arabic-speaking country who seemed to be getting on well with his work, until a colleague of mine got wind from his own student that X was floundering. I asked X to come and see me and show me what he had been doing. It became clear that the 'floundering' was that the student had great difficulty in expressing his thoughts in clear unambiguous English. It appeared that in Arabic how you say something is as important culturally as what you say. The con-sequence was that in writing in English, X had resorted to a flowery style of writing in which all economy of language had disappeared and it became very difficult to tease out the essence of the meaning he was trying to convey. Despite his difficulties he had been too shy to approach me. I was able to help him, at the cost of hours of poring over a text which required not just occasional correction, but substantial re-writing. This case poses the issue of how far a supervisor should correct the English expression of a student's work. With native English speakers, this is not normally a major problem, since the supervisor will only occasionally need to make corrections to the student's spelling and grammar, though the tutor will want to insist on precision and economy of language. With some overseas students, the problem is more important, since if the supervisor is in fact re-writing what the student has written, one might well question how far the thesis is the student's own work. The problem is unlikely to go away, since universities have an intellectual and a pecuniary interest in accepting large numbers of overseas students. Some of the issues concerning the supervision of overseas students are discussed, albeit in an Australian context, by Aspland and O'Donoghue (1994).

Whatever the nature of the lack of communications between

students and their supervisors, it is not possible to guarantee that communication breakdown will never occur. The personalities of the partners in the research process are an element in the situation which it is not possible to control. The least a university can do is to have a statement in the students' guide which indicates that it is expected that supervisors will see their students at a minimum three times a term (or six times a semester) and that records will be kept by the supervisor of all decisions taken at such meetings. But even such statements do not prevent communication from breaking down completely on occasions.

The causes may be trivial or serious. Sometimes, there is a fundamental disagreement between student and supervisor as to how the research should proceed; sometimes the nature of the research has taken an unexpected turn and the present supervisor is no longer the appropriate person; sometimes the student has lost confidence in the supervisor or vice versa; sometimes it is simply a clash of temperaments which make the supervisor/student relationship unviable. Whatever the cause, the institution should have a procedure to cope with such a situation. If the relationship has broken down, then clearly there is no point in the student discussing it with the supervisor. Normally the student should go to the head of his department and indicate what has happened and request a change of supervisor, giving his or her reasons. The head of department will discuss the matter with the student's existing supervisor, who may well agree that a new supervisor is required. The situation may be resolved amicably within the department and a new supervisor allocated to the student. If, however, the situation cannot be resolved at departmental level, then the student may need to take the matter up to a higher level, probably to the dean of research or some such person who is responsible for graduate students. That person will see the student concerned and attempt to find an appropriate supervisor. In fact, when I acted as Coordinator for Research Students in one institution, I was often able to conciliate between a research student and his/her supervisor and no change of supervisor became necessary. Most such problems are dealt with at this or a lower level, but clearly should the issue still remain unresolved then the student must in the last resort be able to appeal to the head of the institution. It may well be that a staff/student liaison committee exists in departments which enable students to air grievances long before they fester and require changes of supervisors.

THE EXAMINATION PROCESS

One of the issues which inevitably arises between student and supervisor is that of the examination of the thesis. First there is the question of when a thesis is ready for presentation. This is not a simple issue of the cosmetic appearance of the thesis as a document, important though this is (see Chapter 6). It is concerned with the adequacy of the thesis as a doctoral dissertation: its power and originality, the importance of the research questions being investigated, and the extent to which the argument is sufficiently backed up by evidence. With experience, a supervisor is able to judge easily enough whether a thesis in its later stages is of such a quality that it will be acceptable for the award of a PhD. In my early days as an inexperienced tutor, I have to admit that there were times when I was unsure. How original has the thesis to be? As Phillips (1994b) states 'there is a range of different ways in which people might be interpreting originality' from doing empirical work that has not been done before, to interpreting existing work in a new way. As indicated earlier, university regulations can be interpreted widely. The importance of the research is largely a matter of its power, that is the kind of impact it makes on existing research and ideas. There are clearly a number of minor problems which require research but which may be dealt with without embarking on a three- to four-year investigation. To a large extent the scale of the investigation should have been decided at the outset and therefore should not arise at the examination stage unless there has been a miscalculation about the importance of the issue being enquired into. On the other hand the extent to which the evidence gathered does or does not test the thesis is crucial. Of course the hunch with which the student started the research may have proved to have been unjustified when the evidence is examined and the main thesis may have a negative rather than a positive finding. This is, of course, not unusual and not a reason for not submitting the thesis.

Sometimes a tutor may be pressurized by a student to allow him/her to submit a thesis or, as indicated earlier, under present conditions when completion rates count as one of the performance indicators for a university's research assessment, the tutor may feel he ought to ensure that a PhD thesis is presented within the normal span of three or four years. My advice to both tutors and students is not to push too hard for early presentation if there is any doubt about the thesis having reached the necessary standard. Whilst it may be possible for a student to be awarded an MPhil instead of a PhD, this is not a very satisfactory outcome for either student or supervisor if the goal has been a PhD.

Assuming that tutor and student are satisfied that the thesis will be ready for submission in the not too distant future, the next stage is deciding on who should examine the thesis. Most universities conform to the Committee of Vice-Chancellors and Principals' recommendations that the supervisor should not be one of the examiners. This is sensible as, however impartial the supervisor may be deemed to be, there is inevitably a feeling that given his or her close association with the student, absolute neutrality of judgement cannot be guaranteed. Both tutor and student will probably know who are likely to be the experts in the field. There is in my view nothing wrong in the tutor discussing with the student who might be the examiners. There are usually two examiners, an internal examiner who is an experienced member of the university where the student is registered, and an external examiner from another university. Once the names of two possible examiners have been decided upon (and a reserve in case the external examiner chosen cannot act), the supervisor may approach the examiners informally to find out whether they would be prepared to act. If both agree then the next step is to submit these names formally to the appropriate university committee for ratification. This is not an automatic process. I have attended many meetings of such committees at which the choice of a particular examiner has been questioned on grounds of his or her suitability given the topic of the research, and another examiner substituted. At this stage, the university will send a formal invitation to the examiners concerned. If both have agreed informally to serve, then they will accept the invitation and the tutor will be informed who will in turn inform the student.

In due course the completed thesis will be sent to the examiners who will be asked to set a date for the oral examination often known as the *viva voce*. The oral examination is something students are often worried about because there is no clear indication of what form it will take or the nature of the interrogation to which the student will have to submit. Indeed Estelle Phillips' research in this area (Phillips 1994b) shows that the student's experience of an oral examination may vary: 'it can last for 45 minutes to 4 hours and can be anything from a friendly discussion to a detailed interrogation.' My own experience, which may not be typical, suggests that the duration may be between one and two hours and that the atmosphere created is likely to be intellectually firm but friendly. Traditionally the purpose of an oral examination was for the student to defend his or her thesis against those who would oppose its conclusions and in some countries the defence of the thesis is carried out publicly. In the United Kingdom it is usual for the oral examination to be carried out in private, the only persons present being the two examiners, the student and often the student's supervisor though s/he may not be allowed to participate in the examination according to some university regulations. Essentially the purpose of the oral examination should be to confirm that the student is able to articulate his or her main findings and to justify these in the light of the evidence accumulated. Thus it is likely the examiners will want to discuss the precise nature of the thesis proposed, the theoretical framework underlying the thesis, the methods used to gather the evidence for the thesis, any treatment of the data statistically (if relevant), the validity and reliability of the data used, the adequacy of the data as a means of testing the thesis, and the possible differing interpretations of the data, and the possible impact of the thesis findings on existing knowledge. The precise nature of the questioning must depend on the nature of the subject of the thesis. A thesis on the work of a French writer such as Roger Martin du Gard will elicit a very different form of questioning from one on the efficacy of the Reading Recovery Method of teaching reading to schoolchildren, or again from a thesis concerned with tracing the influence of postmodernism on urban geography.

In many cases the two examiners will have produced a written report on the thesis prior to the oral examination, giving their preliminary findings and indicating whether they feel the thesis is worthy of a pass. To reassure the candidate, it ought to be said that his or her knowledge of the subject after a three- or four-year period of study for the thesis ought to be superior to that of the examiners, so that if he or she has confidence in the thesis, the oral examination ought to be an interesting intellectual exercise rather than an ordeal. If the examiners in their preliminary reports based on a reading of the thesis agree that it should pass, then unless the oral examination proves disastrous, it will be passed. Sometimes the oral examination turns out to be something of a disappointment for the candidate. I can recall instances in which examiners tended to seize on minor issues of detail for discussion, whilst the main thrust of the thesis is ignored. This ought not to happen. When a student has invested so much time and energy in establishing a substantial proposition, it merits being discussed by the examiners.

The tutor can prepare the student for the oral examination by holding a 'mock *viva voce*' a few days before the date of the examination. Whilst this may be helpful, the student needs to realize that the supervisor can never be sure what the examiners will come up with during the examination.

CONCLUSION

Supervision is a two-way process. It will be successful when both tutor and student have established a good rapport and are reasonably open one with the other. On the one hand the supervisor must establish a climate of confidence in which the student feels s/he can approach the supervisor about any problem met in the course of the research. On the other hand, the student must respond by being willing to share with the supervisor any worries s/he has concerning the research, or indeed any other worries likely to impede the process of the research. Also any differences of views on how to proceed with the research must be discussed as between professionals, always bearing in mind that the ownership of the research is with the student as is the ultimate responsibility for decisions taken.

REFERENCES

Aspland, T. and O'Donoghue, T. (1994) 'Quality in Supervising Overseas Students?' in Zuber-Skerritt, O. and Ryan, Y. (eds) *Quality in Postgraduate Education*, London: Kogan Page, pp. 59–76.

AUT-NATFHE (1993) *Bursting at the Seams*, London: AUT-NATFHE Confederation.

Becher, T., Henkel, M. and Kogan, M. (1994) *Graduate Education in Britain*, London: Jessica Kingsley.

Burgess, R. G., Pole, C. J. and Hockey, J. (1994) 'Strategies For Managing and Supervising the Social Science PhD' in Burgess, R. G. (ed.) *Postgraduate Education and Training in the Social Sciences*, London: Jessica Kingsley.

ESRC (1984) *The Preparation and Supervision of Research Theses in the Social Sciences*, Swindon: Economic and Social Research Council.

O'Brien, P. K. (1995) 'The Reform of Doctoral Dissertations in Humanities and Social Sciences', *Review of Higher Education*, Fall: 4.

Phillips, E. (1994a) 'Avoiding Communication Breakdown' in Zuber-Skerritt, O. and Ryan, Y. (eds) *Quality in Postgraduate Education*, London: Kogan Page, pp. 134–5.

Phillips, E. (1994b) 'Quality in the PhD: Points at Which Quality may be

Assessed' in Burgess, R. G. (ed.) *Postgraduate Education and Training in the Social Sciences*, London: Jessica Kingsley.

SERC (1983) *Research Student and Supervisor: An Approach to Good Supervisory Practice*, London: Science and Engineering Research Council.

Student Programmes Office (1995a) *Doctoral Studies Programme*, London: Institute of Education, University of London.

Student Programmes Office (1995b) *Procedures and Guidelines for Research Students and their Supervisors*, London: Institute of Education, University of London.

Young, K., Fogarty, M. and McRae, S. (1987) *The Management of Doctoral Studies in the Social Sciences*, London: Policy Studies Institute.

Chapter 6

Writing the thesis

James Hartley

INTRODUCTION

How much text have you read this week? And how much have you written? Postgraduate students read and write a great deal. And the kinds of things that they write vary widely. Some items are dashed off without much thought – letters home, reminder notes, etc. Some require more painstaking effort – instructions for participants in an experiment, a poster for a research presentation, or perhaps the introductory chapter for a thesis.

Yet all of these different kinds of writing have one thing in common. Any piece of text is written for a particular audience or reader. And, I suppose, the more you know about your audience – and the more frequently you have done the task – the easier it will be. This, presumably, is one of the difficulties in writing a thesis. Most of us only write one, and we do not often write text fearing that what we have to say might be severely criticized.

There is a large research literature on the topic of academic writing, and I do not propose to review it all here. (I have listed some main references in Appendix 6.1.) My purpose in writing this chapter is to discuss the following topics:

1 How to write clearly;
2 How to revise, or improve the text; and
3 What we can learn about these matters from research on post-graduate writing.

I shall conclude by providing some suggestions for beginning thesis writers.

HOW TO WRITE CLEARLY

Numerous people – writers, researchers, editors – have offered guidelines on how to write clearly (see Appendix 6.1). There are some difficulties with such guidelines for, usually, they are too general. Some people think, for example, that it is not very helpful to be told 'Write short, unambiguous, sentences'. First of all, you are not told how to do it. Next, some variability in sentence length is desirable. Then, if the guidelines get more explicit, it is easy enough to think of exceptions to the rule. And finally, different experts offer different – and sometimes conflicting – advice. Consider, for example, the following remarks:

> Many other writers have offered various suggestions concerning writing style. . . . Although most suggestions seem reasonable, not all are suited to the conceptual article (or thesis). For example, I disagree with several of Dorn's (1985) imperatives: He said, 'Write as you speak' (p. 513). Oral communication does not require the precision of written communication because the speaker receives constant verbal and nonverbal feedback from listeners. Thus do not write as you speak; write with exquisite and exact finesse.
>
> (Salomone 1993: 76)

Whilst acknowledging Salomone's point, I would think that most students would find the advice that he gives – 'write with exquisite and exact finesse' – somewhat alarming.

Nonetheless, despite these objections to guidelines, I happen to think that they can be useful. Guidelines need not be followed slavishly, and they can serve as a checklist or as a reminder of issues that perhaps should be considered. Box 6.1 lists some guidelines for clear writing that postgraduates might find useful.

Box 6.1 Guidelines for clear writing

1 *Keep in mind your reader*
Imagine that you are writing for a fellow student – one who is familiar with the conventions of your discipline, but who does not know your area. This reader needs to be able to grasp what you have done, what you have found out, and to follow your argument without undue effort.

2 *Use simple wording*
Short, familiar words are easier to understand than are technical terms which mean the same thing. Thus it is probably better to

write something like, 'We cannot assume from the start . . .' than it is to say, 'We cannot assume a priori . . .'

3   *Avoid over-using abbreviations*

Many writers abbreviate technical terms: e.g. RAE (Research Assessment Exercise). Text which is full of abbreviations is off-putting. Furthermore, if the abbreviations are unfamiliar, it is easy to forget what they stand for. (I suggest you examine your computer centre literature for typical examples.)

4   *Vary sentence lengths*

Short sentences are easier to understand than long ones. Long sentences overload the memory system. Short sentences do not. However, some variation in sentence length is appropriate as otherwise short sentences get 'choppy'. As a rule of thumb, sentences less than twenty words long are probably fine. Sentences twenty to thirty words long are probably satisfactory. Sentences thirty to forty words long are suspect, and sentences with over forty words in them will probably benefit from re-writing. (The average sentence length of the text in this chapter is, according to my word-processing package, twenty-two words.)

It does not necessarily follow that short sentences are always clear. Many short sentences can turn out to be ambiguous. One of my favourite examples appeared on an application form at Keele as 'Give previous experience with dates'. One candidate wrote, 'Moderately successful in the past, but I am now happily married.'

5   *Use short paragraphs*

Other things being equal short paragraphs are easier to read than long ones. However, as with the suggestion about short sentences, some variation in paragraph length is probably desirable. Nonetheless, it is probably better to err on the side of short paragraphs rather than long ones. Any thesis that has a page of text without at least one new paragraph needs attention!

6   *Use active tenses if possible*

Generally speaking, it is easier to understand text when writers use active rather than passive tenses. Compare the active form, 'We found on these measures that psychologists are more variable than sociologists' with the passive form, 'For the psychologists, as compared with sociologists, greater variation is found on these measures.' My word-processing package seems to suggest (sorry suggests) that I use a lot of passive constructions.

7   *Avoid negatives*

Text is clearer when writers avoid negatives, especially double or treble ones. Negatives can be confusing. I once saw, for example, a label fixed to a lathe in a school workshop which read, 'This machine is dangerous: it is not to be used only by the teacher.' Negative qualifications can be used, however, for particular emphasis, and for correcting misconceptions.

Negatives in imperatives (e.g. 'Do not ... unless ...') are easily understood.'

8 *Place sequences in order*
There are many ways of sequencing text but, whichever way you choose, the presentation needs to have a clear order. It is best, for example, to describe procedures in the order that they take place. For example, instead of saying, 'Before the machine is switched on, the lid must be closed and the paper placed in the compartment' it would be better to say, 'Place the paper in the compartment and close the lid before switching on the machine.'

The following three sentences from *The Patient's Charter* could possibly be better sequenced by putting them in the reverse order:

- The rights and standards set out in this leaflet form *The Patient's Charter.*
- The Charter is a central part of the programme to improve and modernise the delivery of the National Health Service to the public, while continuing to reaffirm its general principles.
- *The Patient's Charter* puts the Government's *Citizen's Charter* initiative into practice in the health service.

Numbers or *bullets* can be used to make a series of points within a paragraph. Thus one might re-write the sentence, 'Four devices to help the reader of a thesis are skeleton outlines for each chapter, headings in the text, a concluding summary and a detailed contents page', as follows:
Four devices which help the reader are:

- skeleton outlines for each chapter;
- headings in the text;
- a concluding summary; and
- a detailed contents page.

It is probably best to use numbers when there is an order or sequence in the points being made. Bullets are more appropriate when each point is of equal value.

9 *Use structural devices to make the organization clear*
Writers can use several devices to help clarify the structure and the sequence of text. Beginning, interim and end summaries can be helpful. Headings in the text label the sections so that writers and readers know where they are and where they are going. Headings help the reader to scan, select and retrieve material, as well as to recall it. Headings can be written in the form of statements or in the form of questions. If the headings are in the form of questions then the text below must answer them, and this helps the reader to follow the argument.

Numbering the headings (and indeed the paragraphs) can also be helpful, although sometimes the numbering of paragraphs can be overdone.

10   *When in difficulty . . .*
If you find it difficult to explain something, think of how you would explain it to someone else. Think of what you would say, try saying it, and then write it down. Then polish this – using the procedures outlined in Box 6.3.

11   *Try reading the text out loud . . .*
Reading the text out loud, or silently to oneself, is an excellent way of seeing how well the text flows. You may find that you need to insert commas to make text groupings clear, that you may get out of breath because sentences are too long, and that you might inadvertently read out a simpler version of the written text. If you do this, change the text to this simpler version.

12   *Ask other people to read your drafts*
Your supervisor may be willing to read drafts, but you will also find it helpful to ask fellow students to read drafts for you. It might be useful to ask them to point out sentences or sections that other readers might find difficult to follow. People are more willing to point out difficulties for other people than admit to having such difficulties themselves.

The nature of writing

It is commonplace, in articles about the nature of writing (e.g. Hayes and Flower 1986: 1107), to divide the processes of writing up into three main, but overlapping, stages:

- *planning* – thinking about the content of the text, and its organization;
- *writing* – putting down one's thoughts on paper – or on screen; and
- *editing* – re-thinking and re-planning, as well as correcting spelling errors and the like.

Skilled writers move constantly to and fro between these stages when writing. And, when writing a thesis, one is likely to use all of these processes when completing sub-parts – such as the abstract, the literature review, the studies to be reported and the discussion.

Some researchers (e.g. Wason 1970: 407) have suggested that in order to improve one's writing skills it is helpful to separate out the three stages outlined above whilst writing. These researchers suggest that during the *planning* stage you should map out the broad issues involved that you wish to cover and the sequence in which you will eventually put them. During the *writing* stage they suggest that you should write as quickly as you can, without paying a great deal of attention to punctuation and spelling, or even completing sentences. *Editing* can follow later, and this stage too can be subdivided. For example, you might edit first for content, then for grammar and style, and finally check the format of the references. Working with word-processors has made these tasks much easier.

Although using word-processors has changed the way that people write (for example, it is harder to talk of writing separate drafts anymore), the basic processes that people use remain much the same. People still plan, write and edit, although perhaps in different proportions than before (Kellogg 1994: 152). This means that some of the findings obtained in earlier studies are still applicable today. In one such study Alan Branthwaite and I used a questionnaire to collect data from eighty-eight highly productive British academic psychologists. Box 6.2 lists the conclusions that we reached, in terms of giving advice for less productive academics and for postgraduate students.

Box 6.2 Characteristic strategies of productive writers in psychology

---

Most productive writers in psychology:

1 Make a rough plan (which they don't necessarily stick to).
2 Complete sections one at a time. (However, they do not necessarily do them in order.)
3 Use a word-processor.
4 Find quiet conditions in which to write and, if possible, write in the same place (or places).
5 Set goals and targets for themselves to achieve.
6 Write frequently – doing small sections at a time – rather than write in long 'binge sessions'.
7 Get colleagues and friends to comment on early drafts.
8 Often collaborate with long-standing colleagues and trusted friends.

Source: Hartley and Branthwaite (1989)

HOW TO REVISE TEXT

Suppose that you have completed the first draft of the introductory section to your thesis, what might you do to improve it? Or, more simply, suppose that a friend gives you a copy of his or her first draft, and asks you to comment on it. What might you do? And is what you might do the same in both situations?

Box 6.3 lists some guidelines for revising text. Again, I hope that these guidelines may be helpful for readers of this chapter. They suggest, as indicated above, that editing is not a simple matter, that it can be subdivided into different components, and that these can be worked on separately. The final point in the list is particularly appropriate for thesis writers. Leaving the text for a while, and then returning to edit once again, is a characteristic of many productive writers. Furthermore, such writers don't just do this once, but several times.

Research on revision suggests that expert writers revise differently from novices (Fitzgerald 1987: 490). Expert writers attend to more global problems (e.g. re-sequencing the content, and re-writing larger chunks of text) than do novices. Novices focus more on changing the wording of the sentences they have produced. It appears that expert writers are better than novices at detecting problems in their texts, and experts are better at deciding what to do about such problems once they have detected them. However, even experts find it harder to detect problems in their own texts than it is to detect them in other people's texts.

Thus this research on revision suggests that it is probably easier to revise someone else's text than it is to revise your own. One reason for this appears to be that people are too close to their own text, and too involved. What has become a commonplace for them can still be very difficult for a reader seeing it for the first time. Hence the value of asking someone else to read and to comment on your text.

In one study of social science postgraduate writers, Torrance, Thomas and Robinson (1992: 163) found that their students fell half-way between this picture of novices and experts described above. Torrance *et al.* reported that these students were prepared to write several drafts, but that they focused more on textual than on global problems.

It may be that writing with word-processors will not help much with global revision when one is writing: it is hard to see the big picture on a small screen. Bem (1995), for example, suggests that one should always print out the whole text in order to facilitate global revisions. Bem puts it thus:

> A word-processor – even one with a fancy outline mode – is not an adequate restructuring tool for most writers . . . don't be ashamed to print out a complete draft of your manuscript; spread it out on table or floor; take pencil, scissors, and scotch tape in hand; and then, all by your low-tech self, have a go at it.
>
> (Bem 1995: 176)

Barzun and Graff also offer a piece of useful advice in this connection:

'Never write on both sides of anything' (Barzun and Graff 1992: 25).

Box 6.3 Some guidelines for revising text

---

1 Read the text through asking yourself:

- Who is the text for?

2 Read the text through again, but this time ask yourself:

- What changes do I need to make to help the reader?
- How can I make the text easier to follow?

3 To make these changes you may need:

- to make big or global changes (e.g. re-write sections); or
- to make small or minor text changes (e.g. change slightly the original text).

You will need to decide whether you are going to focus first on global changes or first on text changes.

4 Global changes you might like to consider in turn are:

- re-sequencing parts of the text;
- re-writing sections in simpler prose;
- adding in examples;
- changing the writer's examples for better ones;
- deleting parts that seem confusing.

5 Text changes you might like to consider in turn are:

- using simpler wording;
- using shorter sentences;
- using shorter paragraphs;
- using active rather than passive tenses;
- substituting positives for negatives;
- writing sequences in order;
- spacing numbered sequences or lists down the page (as here).

6 Keep reading your revised text through from start to finish to see if you want to make any more global changes.

7 Finally repeat this whole procedure some time after making your initial revisions (say twenty-four hours) and do it without looking back at the original text.

Many word-processors come with computer-based writing packages that are supposed to aid writing and revision. A typical example, at the time of writing, is Grammatik 5. This program, when applied to text like this one, highlights possible grammatical, mechanical and stylistic errors (see Box 6.4) and suggests possible solutions. In addition the program provides data such as a word count, and various measures of readability or text difficulty. The problem with such programs, as they currently exist, is that their users have to have a good grasp of grammar to understand whether or not the numerous suggestions offered are valuable, or just 'misunderstandings' on the part of the program. Although I agree that such programs are tedious to use, I personally find them useful. This is largely because they point out (i) the enormous number of long sentences that I write in my initial drafting, and (ii) how many of these sentences are in the passive voice! Certainly simpler programs – like spelling checkers – are invaluable for picking up genuine as well as typing errors.

Box 6.4 A sample of computer programs available in Grammatik 5 from Apple Macintosh

---

Programs which indicate grammatical errors:

adjective errors	object of verb errors
adverb errors	possessive misuse
article errors	preposition errors
clause errors	pronoun errors
comparative/superlative use	sequence of tense errors
double negatives	subject-verb errors
incomplete sentences	tense changes, etc.
noun phrase errors	

Programs which indicate mechanical errors:

spelling errors	punctuation errors
capitalization errors	number style errors
double word	question mark errors
ellipsis misuse	quotation mark misuse
end of sentence punctuation errors	similar words repeated, etc.

Programs which indicate stylistic errors:

long sentences	Americanisms
wordy sentences	archaic language
passive tenses	gender-specific words
end of sentence prepositions	jargon
split infinitives	abbreviation errors
clichés	paragraph problems
colloquialisms	questionable word usage, etc.

RESEARCH ON POSTGRADUATE WRITING

Torrance and Thomas (1994) describe some of the difficulties that social science postgraduates face in writing their theses. They note:

> In addition to lack of appropriate writing skills, students may experience problems when they actually commence writing and become excessively worried by what they perceive to be the demands of the task facing them. The sheer scale of the writing task, for example, may be a source of anxiety and thus procrastination. Similarly some students may be hindered in their writing not so much by an inability to produce good quality text, but by excessive concern as to whether or not what they write is, in fact, in an acceptable style or sounds sufficiently 'academic'. . . . Academic writing for research students may in many ways be similar to any other situation in which a novice has to speak in front of a group of experts, and thus brings with it the same self consciousness and 'fear of saying the wrong thing'. This anxiety may result in writer's block. . . . Worry about correct expression . . . may also present problems for the student if it leads to a premature concern with expression at the expense of content.
>
> (Torrance and Thomas 1994: 106)

Torrance, Thomas and Robinson (1994) described three kinds of postgraduate writer. In their research these authors distinguished between:

- *planners* – students who preferred to have their ideas clear before starting to write, and who produced few drafts;
- *revisers* – students who preferred to start writing first before taking final decisions about content; and
- *mixed* – students who planned but were then forced to change their plans by repeated revising.

Torrance *et al.* report that the 'planners' claimed – in self-report questionnaires – to write more than the 'revisers' and the 'mixed' students. Both the 'planners' and the 'revisers' seemed happy with their writing styles, but members of the 'mixed' group reported more difficulties and anxieties about writing than did the other two groups.

Other investigators have commented on similar differences between individual writers. In the study I mentioned earlier Alan Branthwaite and I distinguished between 'thinkers' and 'doers', and somewhat earlier Lowenthal and Wason (1977: 782) distinguished between 'serialists' who proceeded one step at a time and 'holists' who thought first about the big picture. It is important to note, however, that these may not be enduring personal traits: people's styles of writing vary according to the task in hand. Easy tasks do not require planning, difficult tasks do. And furthermore, these simple labels do not do justice to the variety of writing styles that exist (see Eklundh 1994).

In another study Torrance, Thomas and Robinson (1993) compared three different methods of providing writing instruction for postgraduates. The methods involved were:

1 *A product-centred course.* Here the focus was on rules for producing good writing and on examining standard patterns in academic text.
2 *A cognitive strategies course.* Here the focus was on different strategies for generating ideas and thinking before starting to write.
3 *A generative writing course* – with shared revision. Here the focus was on producing text quickly, and then revising it with colleagues.

The effectiveness of each course was assessed by administering questionnaires to the students involved immediately after the course, and then again some ten to twelve weeks later. In general all three courses were perceived as useful, but the product-centred course was not rated as highly as the other two. After the delay period, the students reported that the generative writing course had been more useful to them than they had originally anticipated. Also at this time the students rated how much thesis-related writing they had done in the ten to twelve weeks interval. Here students who had taken the generative writing course or the product-centred course reported more activities in this regard than did the students who had taken the cognitive strategies course.

Torrance *et al.* concluded that all three courses were effective in different ways. Their results point again to the fact that there are large individual differences in how postgraduates write and, therefore, that there will never be one simple way to make life easier for them.

Finally in this section we may note that although most postgraduates now write with word-processors and – as noted above – these have considerable advantages, they can cause additional difficulties. In a recent survey Reese (unpublished) found that, although all of the twenty-six students in his sample currently produced their work on a word-processor, none of them thought that they had got sufficient training and feedback in information technology skills. These students were very aware that their use of information technology was constrained by what happened to be available – and this included hardware, software and – most crucially – advice. Reese concluded that it should not be left to individual research students to battle against indifference and antagonism to change, and suggested that better training courses were needed. Reese (1996) also noted that the regulations that most students are currently required to follow in order to submit their theses were woefully out of date in terms of information technology.

HELPFUL STRATEGIES FOR BEGINNING THESIS WRITERS

Although we have seen that there are many individual strategies in the ways that postgraduate students set about writing their theses, there are some general strategies that such students might find it helpful to consider. I have listed these as follows:

1 Try to be well organized. Plan well ahead. Try to keep to the plan. (These issues are discussed in Chapters 2 and 4.)
2 Keep notes, files, Xerox copies of materials that may be relevant to your thesis, even if they will eventually be discarded. Some people suggest keeping separate folders for the separate chapters of the thesis.
3 Write from the beginning. Do not leave 'writing up' until the end – you will forget what you did, and why you did it. So keep a written record. With word-processors one can easily add, change, move around or delete words, sentences and paragraphs. If the thesis reports experiments, then early experiments and pilot studies should be written up in full at the time of doing them, even if this detail is not needed in the end.

   Make and keep clearly labelled back-up discs. Inadvertently deleting a chapter you have just written can be soul destroying!
4 Think of how one chapter or other parts of the thesis might be published separately after the thesis is completed. Write them in such a way that it will be relatively easy to do this. After all, few people read theses, so preparing to publish in another format may save you time later on. But don't get distracted. The thesis comes first.

5 Master at the outset the appropriate procedures for presenting text in your discipline, particularly the presentation of footnotes and references. References should be stored – preferably on a database – from the outset in full detail. There is nothing worse than trying to find something that you read several months before just to put the reference in your thesis.

6 Find out the requirements of your institution for the presentation of the thesis. Most institutions, for instance, require the text to be double-spaced, and they specify the width of the margins necessary for binding the thesis. If you prepare your drafts to this specification you will find that you won't make mistakes – like producing tabular arrays that won't fit in. Also, remember that a larger type-size (say 12-point) is necessary on an A4 page to make the text more readable.

7 Regularly submit drafts of sub-sections of your thesis to your supervisor, and ask for guidance on your writing – particularly if you are an overseas student. Also ask your supervisor if there are any books or articles on thesis writing in your discipline or examples of previous theses that can be recommended.

CONCLUDING REMARKS

Generally speaking I have wanted to argue in this chapter that writing is not difficult. We do it all the time in many different contexts. It is the particular context that sometimes makes the task seem difficult. However, if one keeps to the notion of communicating to a reader, separating out the different sub-skills, and using a word-processor to facilitate planning, writing and editing, then the task need not be so alarming. Much of what has been said in this chapter is common sense, and inwardly we know most of it already. The trick is to put into practice what we already know!

REFERENCES

Barzun, J. and Graff, H. F. (1992) *The Modern Researcher*, 5th edn, Orlando, Florida: Harcourt Brace Jovanovich.

Bem, D. J. (1995) 'Writing a review article for Psychological Bulletin', *Psychological Bulletin*, 118, 2: 172–7.

Eklundh, K. S. (1994) 'Linear and non-linear strategies in computer-based writing', *Computers and Composition*, 11: 203–16.

Fitzgerald, J. (1987) 'Research on revision in writing', *Review of Educational Research*, 57, 4: 481–506.

Hartley, J. and Branthwaite, A. (1989) 'The psychologist as wordsmith: A questionnaire study of the writing strategies of productive British psychologists', *Higher Education*, 18: 423–52.

Hayes, J. R. and Flower, L. S. (1986) 'Writing research and the writer', *American Psychologist*, 41, 10: 1106–13.

Kellogg, R. T. (1994) *The Psychology of Writing*, New York: Oxford University Press.

Lowenthal, D. and Wason, P. C. (1977) 'Academics and their writing', *Times Literary Supplement*, 24 June: 782–3.

Reese, R. A. (unpublished) 'Survey of postgraduate student writers' use of computer software', paper available from the author, Computer Centre, Hull University, HU6 7RX.

Reese, R. A. (1996) 'Mistakes, misfits, misprints', *Times Higher Education Supplement*, 17 May, No. 1298 (Research Opportunities Supplement, pp. iv and v).

Salomone, P. R. (1993) 'Trade secrets for crafting a conceptual article', *Journal of Counselling & Development*, 72: 73–6.

Torrance, M. and Thomas, G. V. (1994) 'The development of writing skills in doctoral research students' in R. G. Burgess (ed.) *Postgraduate Education and Training in the Social Sciences*, London: Jessica Kingsley.

Torrance, M., Thomas, G. V. and Robinson, E. J. (1992) 'The writing experiences of social science research students', *Studies in Higher Education*, 17, 2: 155–67.

Torrance, M., Thomas, G. V. and Robinson, E. J. (1993) 'Training in thesis writing: An evaluation of three conceptual orientations', *British Journal of Educational Psychology*, 63: 170–84.

Torrance, M., Thomas, G. V. and Robinson, E. J. (1994) 'The writing strategies of graduate research students in the social sciences', *Higher Education*, 27: 379–92.

Wason, P. (1970) 'On writing scientific papers', *Physics Bulletin*, 21: 407–8. (Reprinted in J. Hartley (ed.) (1980) *The Psychology of Written Communication: Selected Readings*. London: Kogan Page.)

APPENDIX: AN ANNOTATED BIBLIOGRAPHY

Books, papers and chapters on academic writing

Barzun, J. and Graff, H. F. (1992) *The Modern Researcher*, 5th edn, Orlando, Florida: Harcourt Brace Jovanovich.
A classic text on research and writing for literary students but highly informative for all students. There is a useful section on 'The ABC of technique' as well as sections on writing that include: organizing; plain words; clear sentences; quoting and translating; rules of citation; revising; and modes of presentation.

Boice, R. (1990) *Professors as Writers: A Self-Help Guide to Productive Writing*, Stillwater, Oklahoma: New Forums Press.
Lots of help on how to overcome self-doubt, procrastination and writer's block. Includes an annotated bibliography of 100 studies on blocking.

Day, R. A. (1995) *How to Write and Publish a Scientific Paper*, 4th edn, Cambridge: Cambridge University Press.
This is one of the most readable of books of this type. In addition to chapters on how to write the various sections of a paper (e.g. abstract, introduction, method, discussion, etc.) there are succinct accounts of how to present a poster paper, how to write a book review and how to write a thesis. It probably helps to know that Robert Day is a Professor of English!

Hartley, J. and Branthwaite A. (1989) 'The psychologist as wordsmith: a questionnaire study of the writing strategies of productive British psychologists', *Higher Education*, 18: 423–52.
This paper uses cluster analyses to see if there are groups of productive academic psychologists with different writing styles. The analyses suggest that these writers can be distinguished in terms of their approach ('thinkers' versus 'doers') and in terms of their feelings ('anxious' versus 'enthusiastic'). Some prescriptions for improving productivity are provided.

Kellogg, R. T. (1994) *The Psychology of Writing*, Oxford: Oxford University Press.
This book contains excellent summaries of areas of research relevant to this chapter. There are useful accounts of effects of personality variables, different methods of approach, and the effects of word-processors on writing.

Swales, J. M. and Feak, C. B. (1994) *Academic Writing for Graduate Students*, Ann Arbor: University of Michigan Press.
This book is subtitled 'A Course for Non-native Speakers of English', but native speakers can surely profit from it. The text provides exercises which get steadily more involved, starting with writing a paragraph and ending with writing a research paper. All the materials are based on realistic tasks, and are developed from research on academic writing. Students find this text very engaging.

Books/chapters on writing theses

Brown, S., McDowell, L. and Race, P. (1996) *500 Tips for Research Students*, London: Kogan Page.
There are lots of helpful suggestions in this book.

Cryer, P. (1996) *The Research Student's Guide To Success*, Buckingham: Open University Press.
Not quite so much on writing in this text, but one useful chapter in this respect in what is generally a useful text.

Fabb, N. and Durant, A. (1993) *How to Write Essays, Dissertations and Theses in Literary Studies*, London: Longman.
This brief but practical text is probably the standard work for arts students at present. Each of the eight chapters concludes with a summary, a set of specific guidelines and suggested exercises.

Phillips, E. M. and Pugh, D. S. (1994) *How to get a PhD*, 2nd edn, Buckingham: Open University Press.

This book has a useful short section on writing that considers the difficulties facing thesis writers, differences between writers, and offers some practical tips.

Rudestam, K. E. and Newton R. R. (eds) (1992) *Surviving Your Dissertation*,
    London: Sage.
This book contains a chapter on writing which is perhaps more appropriate for arts students. There is an interesting discussion of why people find writing difficult. My psychology postgraduates rate this book as a whole very highly.

Watson, G. (1987) *Writing a Thesis: A Guide to Long Essays and Dissertations*, London: Longman.
A brief book for arts students – not as practical as Fabb and Durant – and somewhat polemical. But it does have a second half which is good on minutiae – quotations, acknowledgements, bibliographies, etc.

Books/papers on features of academic articles

Bem, D. J. (1995) 'Writing a review article for Psychological Bulletin',
    Psychological Bulletin, 118, 2: 172–7.
An entertaining personal account of how to write review articles which has direct relevance to writing the literature review for a thesis. Bem discusses techniques for organizing a review into a coherent narrative, and for giving the readers a clear take-home message.

Hartley, J. (1991) 'Tabling information', *American Psychologist*, 46, 6:
    655–6.
This brief paper discusses, with examples, the difficulties for readers caused by poorly designed tables and poor descriptions of tables in the text.

Hartley, J. (1994) 'Three ways to improve the clarity of journal abstracts',
    British Journal of Educational Psychology, 64, 2: 331–43.
Journal abstracts are notoriously difficult to read. This paper shows how by changing the typography, by using paragraphs to show structure, and by re-writing the text (using the guidelines outlined in this chapter), abstracts in the *British Journal of Educational Psychology* were made much more readable. An appendix gives examples of original and revised texts.

Hartley, J. (1994) *Designing Instructional Text*, 3rd edn, London: Kogan
    Page.
This text develops the argument that the spatial arrangement of a text profoundly affects how one understands it. There are illustrated chapters on this theme, as well as chapters on how to write and revise text, and how to evaluate design decisions. Also included are chapters on the presentation of tables, graphs, forms and questionnaires.

Kosslyn, S. M. (1994) *Elements of Graph Design*, New York: Freeman.
Here a notable psychologist explains step by step how to create clear graphics together with explanations for particular decisions.

Maxwell, S. E. and Cole, D. A. (1995) 'Tips for writing (and reading) methodological articles', *Psychological Bulletin*, 118, 2: 193–8.

This paper highlights how the authors of methodological articles (and chapters) can make their work more accessible to readers who are not methodological specialists.

Rosenthal, R. (1995) 'Writing meta-analytic reviews', *Psychological Bulletin*, 118, 2: 183–92.
Meta-analytic reviews use particular statistical techniques to summarize the results of a large number of different studies on a particular topic. Here the author describes what should typically be included in the introduction, method, results and discussion section of a meta-analytic review.

Simmonds, D. and Reynolds, L. (1994) *Data Presentation & Visual Literacy in Medicine & Science*, London: Butterworth-Heinemann.
This text gives practical advice on the design of tables, graphs, slides and posters, as well as on presentation generally. The text is designed around the Apple Macintosh computer.

Swales, J. and Najjar, H. (1987) 'The writing of research article introductions', *Written Communication*, 4, 2: 175–91.
The authors describe how the introductions to research articles in different disciplines (physics and educational psychology) differ, particularly with respect to whether or not they introduce the principal findings of the studies. Apparently 45 per cent of introductions do this in physics, but only 7 per cent in educational psychology.

Waehler, C. A. and Welch, A. (1995) 'Preferences about APA posters', *American Psychologist*, 50, 8: 727.
This paper presents the results when poster papers were rated in terms of visual display and organization, the role of the presenter, and content. The clarity of the visual display was rated as the most important factor.

Woolsey, D. J. (1989) 'Combatting poster fatigue: how to use visual manner and analysis to effect better visual communications', *Trends in Neuroscience*, 12, 9: 325–32.
This is one of the most detailed treatments of the design of posters that I am aware of.

Chapter 7

Student experiences

Research and the friction of distance

H. W. Dickinson

To say that I drifted into PhD study would not be completely true –
but it would be close. By 1989, the year of my fortieth birthday, I
had an honours degree in English, a masters degree in history and
seventeen years as an officer in the Royal Navy firmly behind me. I
also had a house, a post as a college lecturer in a beautiful area of
the country and, after many years of independence, a wife. My days
of flying from the pitching decks of warships or speeding ashore with
marines were truly over and it was clear that I had finally 'settled
down'. It was equally clear, at least to everybody else, that I had
'fallen on my feet'. Even former service colleagues destined for high
places claimed to be envious of my present position, and the manner
in which it had been achieved.

   In fact, this was only partially true. A settled lifestyle, beautiful
surroundings certainly – but within a matter of months I was
experiencing difficulty at work that seemed to have the potential for
considerable unhappiness. The job itself was quite rewarding. I
enjoyed the teaching, the students were personable and my lectures
were getting good reviews. Yet it was clear that this was not going
to be enough and I became increasingly despondent, particularly at
being unable to influence the shape and structure of things in the
workplace. This left me with what I can only describe as a deal of
'unused energy'. I don't mean that I had any spare time – the system
was adept at filling the working day and beyond and I was frequently
required to work in the evening and at weekends. Yet even at my
most physically exhausted, I was always aware of working below

capacity. It was really this sense of frustration that started me down the path towards a PhD by part-time study.

There seemed to be no shortage of reasons why this was a bad idea. I was already busy at work, my wife was due to have our first baby later that year, our house, which clung precariously to the side of a steep hill, needed major restoration and we were more than four hours from London and the scholarly resources required for such a project. On the positive side, I had a fairly clear idea of the subject area I wanted to explore, I was confident that my former MA supervisor would be interested in the idea and to my surprise, my colleagues, while initially incredulous, were generally supportive.

This period, during which I didn't put pen to paper, was one of the most difficult parts of the whole PhD process. Night after night, often as late as 10 o'clock or after, I would leave work wondering how I could possibly embark on a project that would add a huge amount of work to my already busy schedule. It didn't seem possible. And yet I knew that I couldn't go on just ticking over. In retrospect I realize that I probably agonized over this far too long and that I was overly inhibited about starting something I might not be able to finish. Yet the question was an important one, for I knew my own temperament well enough to realize that, once started, there could be no question of not seeing it through.

I realize that to the outstanding Oxford graduate idly contemplating a further three years amongst dreaming spires, this approach to research must seem pedestrian – but for me it really was datum. By Christmas, some three months after my initial notion, I privately resolved to make a start. The choice of subject was a relatively easy one. I had studied the development of nineteenth-century higher and professional education in England as a component of my master's degree, and my dissertation, on the education of the naval officer in the sailing era, had been derived from this. It seemed natural to expand the topic into the machine age and look at the educational implications of the navy's industrial revolution in the two decades from 1857. In particular I was interested in the impact of new technology on an officer corps still dominated by notions of honour, courage and gentlemanly 'quality' and the extent to which Admiralty educational practice accurately reflected the scientific dimensions of the 'new' navy.

My first task was to determine the extent of existing work in my field, which the experience of my previous degree suggested would be sparse. I checked and re-checked sources and, after some two months or so, concluded that my area of interest was still relatively fallow ground. There appeared to be only one significant contribution – an elderly, unpublished thesis whose author had recently died. Next I tried to determine more closely the dimensions of the topic and identify the central questions to be addressed. Here the lack of any substantial modern study, while in one sense reassuring, was also a recipe for confusion, for there appeared to be no real template for understanding the detail of the subject. Furthermore the evidence was confusing. All the existing works concluded that my period of interest constituted a sort of stasis or quiet interregnum, yet even a brief glance at the primary source material showed evidence quite to the contrary. At first I thought I'd missed some vital point, but the further I probed the more evident the contradiction became. Although I didn't appreciate it at this stage, exploring this paradox was to become the central theme of my work, and I was grateful in the months ahead to have spent this time defining the subject.

My initial research suggested that I would be heavily dependent upon primary material, particularly Admiralty papers deposited in the Public Records Office. The arrangement of these papers and the difficulties they present to the researcher are well known to the extent that the official guide notes that 'the arrangement of the archives in groups and classes does not correspond closely to the original organisation of the documents by the administrations that created them'. It then warns ominously that 'lists appear in many cases to have been drawn up by persons unsure of the origins or nature of the documents they refer to' and finally that 'it is difficult to tell from the lists what the documents contain'. This all proved to be accurate advice and worth bearing in mind when considering any topic dependent on Admiralty papers.

On the positive side there were numerous alternative sources of information, including the Admiralty Library, the National Maritime Museum, the Royal Commonwealth Society, the Royal Naval College at Greenwich and Dartmouth and various collections of family papers. Casting the net wide proved to be profitable for it was soon apparent that certain documents which took days to find at the Public Records Office were easily identifiable and available in other locations. In addition these locations often proved to be more comfortable and less crowded places to work in. After a while I began to get a feel for where information was most likely to be found and although the PRO could seldom be ignored, it gradually moved from being the initial starting point, to the place of last resort.

From the start I was always interested in the question of policy and provision in naval education – the extent to which the Admiralty recognized a problem and tried to do something about it. This meant that official reports, commissions of inquiry and committee findings constituted the bulk of the data I needed and tended to form the way-marks of my work. A cursory glance at the extent of the material in the years I intended to cover convinced me that I needed to reduce the scope of my work and this early decision proved a wise one. Obviously beneath the official picture was a whole sub-strata of data which helped explain why things happened and at which particular moment. Equally, and sometimes vitally, it was necessary to explain why, for no apparent reason, things did not happen at all. Usually the answer to these questions lay in private correspondence, confidential papers, diaries and personal notes. It was in the juxtaposition of the public and private that the particular attraction of the subject lay.

It was about nine months after my initial thoughts that I contacted my former postgraduate tutor, to see if he wanted another PhD student. On reflection this gestation period was time well spent, not least because it enabled me in the initial interview with my supervisor to present my case in a reasonably articulate manner. I felt that, while I certainly didn't know the answer, I did at least have a reasonably close grasp of the question. My tutor seemed to agree and urged me to ponder matters no longer but to produce an abstract and register as soon as possible.

The decision to return to my Alma Mater was a deliberate one, for despite the great distance from home and the logistic problems implied, I particularly liked and felt comfortable in London. I had always found it conducive to study, it was where the bulk of the primary resources were located, and I was familiar with the geography of the town and the university. Perhaps above all, I was keen to work with people I knew and trusted. This was to prove a sound decision, for while I was to be uncertain of a number of things over the course of the project, at no stage did I doubt the guidance of my professor or the support of the department. This was a major factor in bringing the project to fruition.

On the long journey back to the West Country I dwelt on how I would find time to do the work. For most of the teaching year I followed a standard working day, but in the winter we followed a curious split-shift system where I could find myself in the classroom at nine in the morning and still be at the 'chalk face' at seven at night.

As teaching seldom began before nine I decided that the early morning afforded the best opportunity for undisturbed study and devised a routine which saw me at work around 6 o'clock, with the aim of completing three hours writing and researching before the teaching day began. At crucial periods this routine extended into the weekends and was always a feature of the holidays.

This was a pretty punishing routine and, particularly after our new baby arrived in June of my first year, I do remember being quite tired. Two things helped me to handle this and adopt it as standard procedure. First, it was clear that by the end of the teaching day I was tired anyway – regardless of whether I had completed my early morning work. To add anything to the evening would have been inefficient and unsatisfactory in terms of personal relations with friends and family. It was clearly early morning or not at all. Second, shining through the mist of weariness was a real positive sense of achievement. Not only was the research work enjoyable in itself, but it also marginalized many of the concerns about work that had so occupied me just a few months before. Quite simply the whole exercise felt good!

That of course didn't bring the Public Record Office, the British Library or any of the other major sources of primary material any closer to our little country town and I soon had to begin a series of expensive but necessary journeys to London. While it was immediately obvious that library and archive opening hours were hardly designed for the part-time student, I was initially guilty of poor planning. More than once I made a long journey only to find a closed sign and a group of disconsolate fellow researchers standing outside locked doors. It sounds banal, but utterly routine matters such as opening hours, train times, travel costs and special deals on accommodation are a crucial consideration in research planning. A doctorate by part-time study is tough enough without having to deal with the library being closed for stocktaking, or finding that the same ticket is £35 cheaper if booked seven days in advance.

The actual process of examining and using source material went pretty much as I expected, due in part to the experience and practice provided by my master's degree. At an early stage I was surprised to discover that much of the material I required had been filed long before my subject had been administratively identified, with the result that I was condemned to wander through large collections of papers merely classified as 'promiscuous' or 'miscellaneous'. Here there was obviously a requirement for patience, but also for the discipline to resist spending hours browsing happily through material utterly irrelevant to the matter at hand. Otherwise I think my experience with primary sources was common to most students – being roughly divided between identifying that important clue, or more commonly acknowledging that a vital piece in the jigsaw cannot be found! Success seemed to depend as much on tenacity and resilience as on any particular inspiration or insight.

As a part-time student, separated from primary sources by a three hundred mile journey, I had to adopt a fairly rigid division of labour. Holidays were used for the identification and examination of documents and the early morning routine during term time for collation, assessment and production of the thesis. The arrangement was generally successful although it depended heavily on photocopying – a time consuming and expensive pastime – but one to which I could see no real alternative. I soon learnt that it was false economy to skimp on this process, for that discarded page inevitably turned out to be the vital one!

Quite early on in the research process I faced the usual dilemma of how to write up the information. Was it preferable to make notes, cover the spectrum of the topic and then write the account? Or should one attempt to proceed sequentially, dealing with a section or a topic at a time, writing up as one went along? Clearly for the part-time student there were pit falls in both approaches. On the one hand one could be left after a number of years with little more than a pile of notes, or alternatively, several chapters could be completed only for the theories and conclusions therein to be contradicted by later investigation. In the end I opted for the latter method and wrote up as I went along. This was generally successful, partly, I have to admit, because I was lucky but also because of the time spent in the pre-registration period working with the overall shape of the work. Largely without realizing it, I probably had a better grasp of the topic than I knew at the time.

Writing up went relatively smoothly. I undertook the work chapter by chapter, starting with the introduction and continuing in sequence. As each section was completed I posted it to my supervisor in draft form with an explanatory letter. On return I adapted and amended until I was satisfied, and then placed it to one side before commencing the next section. Of course each chapter posed its own individual challenge which in turn dictated completion time. This varied, for a 12,000 word piece, from about four months to almost a year. In addition to our exchange of letters I tried to see my supervisor for a tutorial once every nine months. These were immensely useful and constructive sessions which both adjusted the focus of the work and injected impetus towards completion.

I had been warned before starting that a doctorate by part-time study might be a lonely business and that I should consider joining an advanced studies group or research society where common problems might be discussed and resolved in the company of fellow students. While this seemed logical enough, and the university and students' union certainly provided plenty of support in this area, I found myself taking rather the opposite course. Surprisingly, I discovered that to some extent I enjoyed the isolation of the research process and that I had no desire to seek out others, recount my experiences or indeed listen to anyone else's! For me much of the attraction in the work was derived precisely from a sense of confronting and solving problems myself. I don't doubt that I made a rod for my own back in this matter but I think it is important to trust, have faith in your own instincts and above all adopt an approach that produces results.

About half way through my fourth year I was nearing the end. By now I felt I had drafted a reasonably coherent re-interpretation of historical events and was ready to explain the relevance of the work to wider issues, via a conclusion. I also felt optimistic and confident that I would soon be finished, for my writing skills had steadily improved and the penultimate chapter had been completed in record time. I was aiming for a compact conclusion of perhaps no more than twenty-five pages and was certain that in a matter of weeks it would be done. Yet even at this stage the PhD process was capable of surprise, and it was to be a long and difficult four months before I finally pulled together the ideas and reasoned them into a set of tempered arguments. The stumbling block was my part-time status. I simply couldn't devote enough time exclusively to the work without being interrupted and distracted by other matters. I eventually overcame this by moving into a hotel room and not returning home until the work was finished!

And so the project was completed. It had taken just under five years and throughout that time I had laboured more or less continuously, seldom leaving the work untouched for longer than a week or ten days. I had worked hard. I had also been fortunate, particularly in the quality of the supervision and the support of my family. My personal circumstances changed over the time – my parents-in-law died, my father suffered a stroke and, on a happier note, our two children were born – all things which, together with the pressures of a full-time job, tested my resolve. Nevertheless, I cannot recall anything approaching a 'crisis'. I didn't encounter a 'block' or suffer any particular source of doubt and at no stage did I consider giving up. I do remember times when it resembled a fight and, particularly towards the end, I seemed to be involved in an almost physical struggle. Most of all, however, my PhD story was one of considerable and often intense pleasure. In a sense it was born out of frustration but it rapidly became the most satisfying and challenging of experiences. I recommend it!

Researching, moving and other facets of daily life: Undertaking a PhD as a mature student
Helen Connell

WHY DID I CHOOSE TO DO A PhD?

I grew up as the youngest in a university family in Australia, and although I happily studied at undergraduate level, I was determined not to follow in the footsteps of my siblings and parents and become a university-based researcher and teacher – my then limited image of the options open to PhD graduates. After my first degree I spent a number of years working and travelling in different countries before returning to Sydney. During these years I surprised myself somewhat by collecting a teaching certificate in London and a master's degree in Ottawa.

Having to this point studied in various fields of geography, and being intent on working in planning, I found myself offered a very interesting job in curriculum development – an aspect of educational planning, as it were. I worked for three years in Sydney and then Canberra as project officer helping establish a new international educational consortium in the Pacific region, developing curriculum ideas and resource materials with an international and Pacific outlook for schools.

By the time my contract had finished in 1980, I had mapped out and begun work on a PhD (by thesis only), using as a focus the process of establishing the Pacific Circle Consortium. What attracted me to embark on this study, and reverse my earlier resolve to avoid doctoral studies, is hard to say with any certitude – such decisions are usually complex and many factors come into them. One thing was absent, however, and that was the idea that a PhD would be a meal ticket. A strong motivating factor was certainly the wish to come to grips with a defined substantive body of knowledge and to develop my critical and creative faculties – essentially reasons to do with personal development. My interest in doctoral study emerged in my early thirties as the result of experiences in adult and working life.

CHOOSING A RESEARCH TOPIC AND DECIDING HOW TO APPROACH IT

My research topic, then, emerged rather naturally from work in which I had been engaged for a few years. I had been closely involved from the start with the creation of the Consortium – effectively a grouping of educational institutions including universities, independent research and development institutes, and government departments from several countries of the Pacific Rim, established under the aegis of the Centre for Educational Research and Innovation at the Organisation for Economic Co-operation and Development. I had been party to early plans, subsequent modifications, and the realities of development work as part of a multinational team operating from different and distant institutional bases.

Thus, at the outset I had a specific activity which I wished to study in depth, but I had an open-ended and exploratory rather than closed and tightly defined set of questions to ask. I wished to understand the evolution of the activity – why it took this particular form, what its strengths and weaknesses were, what problems it had encountered, how these had been addressed, and the broader issues arising for educational policy and practice. I thus had an interpretive objective and needed to draw strongly – though not exclusively – on material in the subjective realm.

There were several sources of data for the study. First, documents of different sorts – publications, draft materials (often in several versions), correspondence, meeting reports, meeting notes. Second, the perceptions and experience of the participants. Third, observation of the Consortium in action, particularly during the annual meetings. Fourth, systematic reflection on my own involvement and intuitive understanding of the activity. Fifth, literature documenting other comparable activities and enabling the Pacific Circle experience to be placed against various forms of educational knowledge. Set out in this way these data sources seem clear and straightforward. But mastery of them was another matter for reasons that I give below.

RESEARCH AS JUST ONE DIMENSION OF LIFE: FITTING PhD STUDY IN WITH OTHER THINGS

Absorbing as library study, interviewing and writing can be, PhD research for a mature student is generally only one dimension of life, which has to take its place alongside other interests and responsibilities. I found my PhD became something of a continuing project done in fits and starts over a period of years, and which followed rather than led family activities.

I started my PhD in 1980 as a full-time student on a government scholarship at the Australian National University in Canberra, but eighteen months later my husband moved to a job in London. Rather than remain a further eighteen months to complete my studies full time in Canberra (which was what was required under the then statutes of the ANU), I chose to join my husband in London, withdrawing my candidature from the ANU. I enrolled in 1982 on a part-time basis for a PhD with the London University Institute of Education where a tradition of much greater flexibility for organizing study prevailed. I needed to recast my research proposal to make it relevant to a new setting in the northern hemisphere, but was able to maintain the centrality of the case study of the Pacific Circle Consortium, and therefore to use the materials I had collected during my first period of study in Canberra.

Our stay in London saw us buying a house in much need of renovation, and my husband and I did a considerable amount of the work ourselves over the next few years. This was interesting and rewarding, but very time consuming. My desk for two years was on the upstairs landing, surrounded variously by removed floorboards, items to be restored or painted, and periodically under considerable layers of dust associated with different aspects of the renovation project. Eventually I had a most elegant study overlooking our by then well-developed back garden – but that was some time on.

Once in London, I no longer had a scholarship for study, and although I was fortunate to have a husband who was able and willing to support my studies financially, I wished to continue to make at least some contribution to family coffers. So, during the remainder of my doctoral studies I worked part-time on a consultancy basis. Thus, the reality of 'mature age' study is that it is not uncommon –

indeed it is probably the norm – to have accumulated various responsibilities as part of a family and as part of a work team, around which study needs to be slotted. What is more, it would have been foolish to neglect the rich cultural opportunities of life in London and time had to be made available for theatre, galleries and regular forays into the countryside.

During the period when I was studying full-time in Canberra, I had considerable contact with other PhD students, as we all had desks in a small house on the campus. This proved a congenial, research-focused environment, although because of the wide variety in our topics, our research activities were essentially independent. With the move to London, however, the university life of the campus, which had featured strongly in all my university studies to that point, became no longer of prime importance. In London my study base was at home; I had no desk at the university, and visited the campus only for specific library research, for arranged meetings with my supervisor or for the occasional seminar.

Working from a home base is a particular challenge as it requires the discipline of lengthy periods on a regular basis dedicated to study, and not allowing oneself to be diverted by the constant multitude of domestic requirements of shopping, cooking and cleaning, not to mention the more pleasurable pursuits of listening to radio programmes, visiting neighbours and getting involved in community activities. I tried to block out regular hours each morning for study and schedule other things in the afternoon – but there were often times when I had to be flexible and vary this arrangement, particularly in relation to the demands of my consultancy work. Evenings and weekends are never sacrosanct when one's study base is at home, and especially when studying on a part-time basis.

Efficient time management, then, is a central part of the art of mature study. For me, parenthood came later, though for many it is another dimension of the day to day reality of graduate level studies. The mature student has many advantages, not least a definite sense of purpose and experience in managing competing demands. Even so, I never found it easy to balance so many demands and opportunities.

Part-time study over a period of years can become a way of life, so that I found it quite useful to have a deadline for finishing my thesis. My husband changed job again, entailing a move back to Australia at the end of 1985, and this was the deadline I met for finishing my studies.

COLLECTING THE DATA

During my first year and a half of doctoral study in Canberra I collected the bulk of the documentation I needed on the Pacific Circle Consortium. One of the participating organizations was based in Canberra and this provided ready network access to the other member organizations.

From its inception in 1977 the Pacific Circle Consortium held annual meetings, and given that I had no research funding for travel to member institutions (a common constraint on PhD research), attending these meetings provided the best (and most economical) opportunity to interview the full range of participants, and to observe the Consortium in action. During my study period I went to two annual meetings (Sydney and Hiroshima) – essentially at my own expense, though with some costs subsidized.

As many of the participants were also personal friends with whom I had worked on the project in its initial years, I encountered no resistance to setting up interview schedules – my main constraint was time. The Annual Meeting schedules were always very full, so I necessarily had to timetable interviews into the interstices – whenever and wherever possible. This meant that the detail of interviews was rather variable, and I needed to establish additional mechanisms to seek information from participants. What is more, friendship can temper objectivity. It was necessary to formalize interviews and to establish a 'distance' between interviewer and interviewee.

I decided not to tape record interviews, but rather to take brief notes and expand on these soon after each interview – for me it was the interpretation, not the exact form of words which was important. Following completion of the interviews with individual participants, I wrote an account of the participation of each of the then nine member institutions (drawing on multiple sources), and then sent the relevant account to each of my interviewees for their comments, corrections and amplifications. As I was operating within a strong friendship network, and engaged on a study which was viewed as valid and useful by Consortium members, I had a very good response to this. Fortunately for my research, the Pacific Circle Consortium proved to be an innovation which has continued (and is indeed still functioning after twenty years), so that during my time in London I was able to update developments, and verify interpretations without great difficulty.

The process of systematically reflecting on my own experience and that of close colleagues as participants in the Consortium involved a conscious stepping back from the characteristic advocacy engagement which participants have with the various projects and programmes they are working on. The lens for viewing actions must be a critical and dispassionate one. There is, however, the added dimension in reviewing one's own experience as participant observer of having an intuitive understanding of the events. This privileged 'insider' dimension to my understanding was a valuable asset, but one which had to be handled with considerable care. Passing draft materials to 'critical friends' is a useful corrective to the inevitable subjectivism of this kind of study.

THOSE WHO HELPED GET IT FINISHED

As I had no coursework requirements for my PhD, my main formal university contact was with my supervisors. At the ANU I had joint supervisors from different parts of the university, because there was no education faculty, and the nature of the topic I had chosen did not fit neatly into any single existing academic grouping. Once I had negotiated the topic and research plan with my supervisors, and had been accepted as a candidate by the university, it was up to me to get on with the work. I met on an occasional basis with my supervisors to discuss progress and presented a seminar on my research plan during my eighteen months there.

When I enrolled at the London Institute of Education, as before, after negotiating the topic, research plan and timetable with my supervisor, it was up to me to continue the research. I did not have a pattern of regular meetings, but essentially, worked on my own at home until I had some draft material for comment – and then arranged to discuss it. This lack of regular requirements from the university suited me, as it made it easier to balance my various commitments, but it meant that the onus was on me to keep the research moving. I found the role my supervisor played of critical friend worked well. Frank and constructively critical discussions of my attempts to develop coherence in the body of research material were, I found, invaluable in helping tighten the framework and sharpen the argument of the thesis for the next draft. While this 'crafting' stage of the thesis was – or at least *seemed* – quite long (it overlapped with the continuing process of data gathering and inter-pretation), I found it to be one of the most interesting and valuable learning elements of my doctoral studies.

My husband provided much valued moral support, but in addition I had the unusual circumstance of substantive professional critiques from him on my work. He had, like me, been closely involved in the establishment of the Pacific Circle Consortium in his job in Canberra, so throughout the period of my studies I was able to discuss the evolution of my thinking with him, and he gave extensive comments on draft material.

Other assistance came throughout from library staff, academic friends and members of the Pacific Circle Consortium whose interest provided a stimulus to complete the study. Thus, while the ultimate responsibility for completing a PhD thesis is the candidate's, my experience suggests that professional and personal support have a vital role to play.

Towards a thesis

Jane Savage

As I write this I am undertaking the final rewriting of my thesis after several drafts. It feels as if it is at the penultimate stage in producing the final polished thesis. In personal terms my progress and, at other times, lack of progress have mirrored events that have occurred in the rest of my life and for me the breakthrough has been recognizing this, and organizing my thesis work accordingly by not trying to ignore the fact that certain events were not conducive to study.

I started my first attempt at personal research into primary science before I took up my post as a lecturer in primary education. Combinations of events, including a poorly thought-out research idea, irregular meetings with my supervisor and a change of job from a deputy headship in a primary school to the lecturing post at the Institute of Education, University of London, made my progress frustratingly slow. My study and research preparation was haphazard and lacking in direction. Many of these difficulties stemmed from the limitations of my research proposal. My initial ideas relating to my interest in assessment in primary science were too broad conceptually and based on very limited work which had been undertaken in my own classes in primary schools. At the time the existing theoretical base was limited and I became confused when reading some of the more general texts on research methodology and general assessment which were mostly more concerned with older children and their work. I could not clearly relate this more generalized reading to the work that I had already undertaken and more importantly what I wanted to research in the future. I had no clear picture of how my research should proceed. However, events which accompanied the introduction of the National Curriculum and its associated assessment procedures which were introduced in the late 1980s made many of the practical strategies that I had been exploring of limited relevance to the new imposed assessment procedures. Instead of thinking clearly about what exactly it was within the area of science assessment that I was interested in, I attempted to mesh my previous reading and practical work with changing events. This approach did not work mainly because I was still unclear about the direction of my research and where I wanted it to lead.

Then in 1992 I was offered a remarkable opportunity but one which also necessitated a change in my area of study and to a great extent my work within the university. For two and a half years I was seconded from my post as a primary lecturer to be the research officer for an ESRC (Economic and Social Research Council) funded project into school development planning in primary schools. This project was directed by Professor Peter Mortimore and Barbara MacGilchrist. Another colleague, Charles Beresford, was a research associate. At the time that the research project started, Peter Mortimore, now director of the Institute of Education, was deputy director of the Institute of Education, University of London and Barbara MacGilchrist was head of in-service training at the Institute. Charles Beresford was an ex-inspector from Cambridgeshire and a freelance educational consultant. The change of subject area was a big decision. I was moving from an area where I had considerable experience and growing confidence as well as a real enthusiasm for the subject and my work with students at all levels to one which was much more unfamiliar. However it was also an opportunity and one which I do not regret taking.

The aims of the project were to:

1 Carry out an empirical investigation of the implementation and impact of school development plans in primary schools in order to provide a contribution to knowledge in the form of a clear and detailed description of an innovative development.
2 To examine how the findings of the study can contribute to the theories of how change takes place in schools and in particular to strengthen the link between school effectiveness and school improvement theory and practice.
3 To identify good practice and, if appropriate, to disseminate this to policy makers and practitioners.

We sought to investigate if school development plans had an impact on the management of the school as a whole, on classroom management, on the professional development of teachers and on the learning opportunities for teachers (Hargreaves and Hopkins, 1994).

Through the guidance of Professor Mortimore we were careful to set the project up so that the other three of us who were working on our theses had linked but separate foci of study. My particular area has been focused on the classroom teachers within the schools we were researching. We also had common supervisors who were not so closely bound up with the day to day operation of the project and who co-supervised us with Professor Mortimore.

The research team had regular, mostly weekly, team meetings to discuss the progress of the project. In addition we worked together on pieces of writing for a varied range of audiences, conference presentations and most importantly on the research instruments for the semi-structured interviews, classroom observations and other evidence collection which formed the basis of the data pool for the research. We also shared and discussed reading and research methodology and brought our individual strengths and areas of interest and expertise to the project as a whole. These elements together with regular tutorials with my supervisor formed the basis of my research training. At all stages, I was as interested in observing and reflecting on the process of supervision as I was in the specific discussions and advice that I was offered. I was and continue to be fortunate to have had this talented, experienced support. In many ways the supervision with its combination of pressure and support could not have been bettered.

The work was intense, the workload high and the levels of support and intellectual debate stimulating. The day to day organization of the project also meant that I had considerable autonomy. There were certain things that held back progress. One was the fact that all the classroom and the bulk of the school data collection in all nine schools that we were studying was done by me. This limited the time we could spend in each school. It also curtailed certain aspects of data collection, such as interviewing pupils, which we would have liked to have included. Another was my lack of detailed training in using data analysis programs such as SPSS. I resented the time it took to get good quality training both because time was so short and because it detracted from the more interesting business of collecting and analysing the data. Then when I was familiar with parts of these programs the process of loading the data was enormously tedious.

Some of the other research training on general methodological issues that was on offer was not very helpful. In many ways as a team we were operating at a specialized and different level.

As the person with the main responsibility for the data collection and analysis I was guilty of letting the project take over time which should have been more closely guarded for my personal writing. However, by the summer of 1994 I had written up a draft thesis of over 90,000 words which comprised the bulk of the data collected and the main body of my thesis. By the time the project officially ended in the same summer and the final report had been submitted we were also well into drafts of the book of the project which was published soon after (MacGilchrist *et al.*, 1995). I felt exhausted but also much clearer about the nature of funded research, at least on this project, recognizing the importance of skills and attitudes such as organization, efficiency, stamina and determination, and also recognizing that some aspects of the data collection, analysis and the day to day management of the project as a whole were both essential and boring. Some of the mystique and high status of research work within the university had been exploded, whilst the enormous thrill of patterns emerging from the data and of working with the schools and with such a talented research team were a revelation.

With hindsight I now realize that I could have not kept working at this pace for much longer. Stressful personal events such as the end of my marriage had occurred without any real time or will being devoted to coming to terms with them. Soon after the project's final report was filed and our latest presentation to the research community had taken place, I took a three week holiday with my family and new partner to explore my father's childhood in India. On my return I realized more clearly how I needed to find more effective ways to combine my thesis and the rest of my life. I wanted both, not one or the other. The next eighteen months were a time of consolidation. I worked on reading and trying to get the key themes of my thesis sorted out so that it became more separate from the project as a whole and also had a clear story to tell. We completed the book of the project and I had a break from full-time work at the university as I had my baby daughter.

Only now, when my life is more settled and having made the decision to return to work part time to enable me to spend time with my daughter and to work on the completion of my thesis, do I feel able to face the task of finally pulling this piece of work together. Now I feel more personally motivated and in control of the process.

The external pressures to complete before this have not always been productive, for me the motivation has to come from within and now my reasons for wanting to complete are different. The partial break from the thesis when I continued to read and redraft the structure and content of the thesis helped me to clarify what I can assert and back up with evidence, and what is more unclear or not so pertinent to my story.

My enthusiasm has grown as my personal ownership has increased. Whilst I am clear that the story of the development of my thesis so far is not an ideal model, strengths have come from the difficulties which I have both constructed and encountered. The professional respect that I have for my supervisor and research colleagues has grown enormously. In many ways as I look forward to the completion of my thesis I feel privileged to have made the journey so far in such distinguished company and now finally in a manner where the personal and the professional are more in balance.

REFERENCES

Hargreaves, D. H. and Hopkins, D. (eds) (1994) *Development Planning for School Improvement*, London: Cassell.

MacGilchrist, B., Mortimore, P., Savage, J. and Beresford, C. (1995) *Planning Matters. The Impact of Development Planning in Primary Schools*, London: Paul Chapman.

MacGilchrist, B., Savage, J., Mortimore, P. and Beresford, C. (1994) 'Making a Difference', *Managing Schools Today*, 3(9): 7–8.

Chapter 8

Intercultural issues and doctoral studies

Jagdish Gundara

INTRODUCTION

This chapter will consider three issues with reference to interculturalism and doctoral work within British universities. The first
issue is that of the attributes of and attributions to students who
undertake doctoral work. Certain dynamics affect students from
socially diverse backgrounds who undertake doctoral work either as
part-time or full-time students, and the common sense but un-
considered labels which are used about these students and their
studies. The inter-relationships between different groups and types
of students also require debate.

The second issue is that of the doctorate itself and the institutional attributes in relation to the culture of the university and
the cultures of the diverse students who undertake doctoral research.
While there may be some crude forms of racism, more frequently
much more subtle ways exist by which, for instance, women students
tend to be excluded from doctoral studies. The third issue concerns
the attributes and attributions in relation to knowledge which have a
bearing in intercultural contexts. The position argued in this section
is that a Eurocentric curriculum detracts from genuinely intercultural
doctoral work of a high academic standard. Critics of intercultural
education assert that it leads to a lowering of standards. However, in
this section it is argued that academic standards can only be
considered to be rigorous if doctoral studies are genuinely intercultural. It is the current Eurocentric basis of knowledge itself which
is a bar to high academic standards and a diminution of imagination,
vision and original doctoral work.

ATTRIBUTES AND ATTRIBUTIONS: STUDENTS AND DOCTORAL STUDIES

The academic community is constituted of different groups, disciplines and domains and in principle the presence of culturally different groups and the knowledge they bring should not be seen as presenting any problems. There are, however, a range of questions arising from social inequalities endemic within ethnic differences and minority status which have a bearing on higher education institutions.[1] The first is that of differentials in access to higher education from different communities. These differentials lead to lower levels of take-up at doctorate levels by students from marginalized sections of the society. Students from these communities may not only have low levels of representation within the student body but also have higher proportions studying technical and business subjects and fewer in the pure sciences or in the arts and humanities – the higher status curriculum subjects.

This is not simply a correlation between different academic cultures and those of the so-called ethnic groups and minority communities. Attitudes, experiences and perceptions of learning, for instance from middle-class Asian and Afro-Caribbean families, may have much in common with those from middle-class English families. On the other hand, the differences in attitude between middle-class and marginalized sections of the (British) communities in relation to higher education may be great. Academic institutions at formal and informal levels of their functioning may need to take measures which diminish cultural distances between marginalized sections of Afro-Caribbean, Asian and British communities and improve institutional access for students from these groups. At one level friendly and supportive relations between staff and students may help to bridge some aspects of cultural distance for all students in higher education.

There may, however, also be institutional customs, practices, procedures which overtly and covertly discriminate against students from racially and culturally different backgrounds. At this level formal policies might need to be enacted to ensure that institutional arrangements and practices do not discriminate against groups defined as being different. A monitoring of such policies ought to ensure that student admissions, staff appointments and promotions are transparent. This is essential both for the optimum functioning of higher education institutions and in ensuring quality control in relation to equity in higher education.

One of the positive aspects of a diverse student body at doctoral level is that students bring different ways of behaving and interacting with each other and their tutors. Some students may be reticent; openness on the part of staff can allow them to engage with members of the faculty and other students. However, in certain Asian and African cultures appropriate behaviour towards those who are learned and academic is to demonstrate respect and to maintain what is seen by them as a proper distance. The hierarchical character of an academic institution in certain cultures prevents some students in Britain from treating members of the faculty informally or challenging statements made by staff, even if that is the norm in Britain.

Where the academic and support staff are from non-majority backgrounds themselves, this may enable the student to fit into an academic milieu more congenially. An intellectually and materially supportive environment is a prerequisite to establishing collegiality. A structured orientation programme is also of great importance. This enables students to meet each other, the faculty, support staff, and to understand the structure of the institution, so that they can engage personally with the institutional culture. Such an orientation programme is not only useful for out-of-town students, but is especially useful for students from overseas, who have little understanding of British society, its culture and its institutions. Such students generally feel lonely and need friends to begin to feel familiar with the place and the people.

The orientation programmes of some North American universities perform an excellent role in ensuring that there is a collegial, friendly and welcoming postgraduate community. Such an orientation in no way detracts from the academic nature of doctoral studies or the intellectual rigour expected of students who attend these institutions.

The traditional British model of doctoral work, which used to rely on autonomous student research without necessary participation in additional course work, can be a solitary experience for those students who are from out of town, belong to minority communities or are from overseas. Such students normally receive assistance from their tutors soon after beginning their studies to help design their study programmes, prepare collection of data and analysis as well as developing their writing skills. However, many students would benefit from advice on a range of matters, which, though unrelated to the strictly academic issues, would enhance their performance.

This kind of supportive structure can enable students to actualize their scholarly contribution and optimize their academic potential, thereby lowering the number who fail to complete their doctoral studies.

Special problems are presented by those who have to undertake doctoral work on a part-time basis. While the desire to learn and to become academically qualified is very high amongst certain categories of students, they typically have complex living circumstances. Some may have full-time jobs and families but, nevertheless, may wish to improve their professional qualifications and future prospects. If they are more mature than other students and some staff members, then delicate handling may be necessary. However, most university faculties are not organized to deal with the specific needs and support requirements of such students. Some of these students find a great deal of difficulty in orienting themselves towards a learning situation after long absence from educational institutions. Though their supervisors may have very high expectations of the students themselves it may be extremely difficult to acquire the intensive high levels of reading, writing and learning modes required for doctoral work. This is particularly a problem if such students are researching into fields which are totally unrelated to their full-time jobs. For instance, a history teacher might find it easier to write about teaching history in an intercultural way, but may be undertaking a more difficult dissertation on questions of epistemology in relation to the curriculum, or an examination of the historiography of the subject as an intellectual issue. It is only the most committed and motivated who would undertake the challenge of shifting from their field of work to another one for their doctoral work. For such students, attendance at conferences, courses or seminars can provide contacts with other students and academics which represent an important way of inculcating and inducting part-time students into the culture of doctoral research.

The involvement of women from minority communities presents a rather different set of potentials and problems. Such students may be even more motivated than some men from their communities and are perhaps more disciplined and committed. Their focus and concentration may partly arise from their involvement with carrying out chores in their personal capacities at home and they may not take education for granted. Such a situation may not only provide the impetus to learn but also a personal discipline in undertaking and completing tasks. In certain cases they may, however, have a lower order of academic skills and knowledge resulting from the in-adequacies of the previous learning institutions they may have attended.

Ideally faculties taking on women students from diverse back-grounds should create a friendly academic structure to enable students in intercultural environments to make intellectual contribu-tions at conferences, lectures and seminars. This can in turn ensure a supportive context in which students from minority backgrounds can make positive intellectual contributions. Such a structure ought to enable students who are expressing different views to be confident and comfortable in doing so. Different perspectives developed by these students can enrich the pool of ideas all doctoral students are exposed to and can help in raising levels of intellectual discourse amongst a particular cohort.

As stated earlier, some students from certain minority com-munities and women in particular may feel deferential towards their tutors and there may be various reasons for this. Tutors' perceptions and students' own responses may not cohere, and tutors need to be sensitive to the different value system that such students might bring. These divergent values may be beneficial in broadening the ways in which faculties operate and doctoral students are supervised. When students have low levels of confidence during certain periods of their research tutors need to demonstrate support in improving their confidence. In certain cases students may lose confidence either because they perceive the poor quality of their own work or because of misunderstandings arising for cultural reasons. It might be dif-ficult for such students to re-acquire the capacity to produce work of desirable quality unless the problems are resolved quickly. In addition to the direct role of the tutor, s/he should also facilitate student collaboration. A cohort of students may be able to support each other's work, particularly if there are problems of cultural distance.

INTERACTIONS BETWEEN CATEGORIES OF STUDENTS

The differences between home and overseas students is in itself a complex issue. The complexities are reflected in the way in which students from the European Union countries may be seen to be closer to home students because of the British proximity to Europe. But paradoxically, they may be more distant than doctoral students from the Commonwealth who, because of former colonial links, can work in English. Such students may also have an understanding of the British university system based on their experiences in universities which have been developed on the British model. Both these groups of students may have varying levels of competence in English or might be familiar with different types of English. A major challenge for higher education institutions is to build upon the different knowledge systems and intellectual understandings that both these categories of students bring. The problem of language will be discussed below, but tutors need to acquire competence to draw upon the different modalities of thinking, conceptual frameworks and knowledge which students from diverse backgrounds bring.

The differences between home and overseas students can also emerge in another way. This is partly a result of universities earning a higher rate of fees from overseas students and accepting students with large scholarships or from wealthy families. Such a practice can lead to tensions between all home (whether from minority or dominant communities) and overseas students. The resentments of home students can create more problems for overseas students, resentments which are inimical to the mutual support systems and structures which overseas students require. In such situations home students, whether white or black, may alienate the overseas students. Where home students are white and overseas students are not, then racial tensions may be increased, thus negating positive aspects of intercultural learning and connections. Such tensions may also put to the test institutional mechanisms to deal with xenophobia and racism when these arise.

These resentments can be especially exacerbated if overseas students with lower academic qualifications than those required for home students are accepted to carry out doctoral research. In such cases, it is important to ensure that, before overseas students embark on formal doctoral work, they receive appropriate preparation in spheres and types of competencies to enable them to function effectively. Such preparation can also help address certain weaknesses in research skills that students may have acquired from institutions with pedagogies different from those of British universities. For instance, some South Asian students take for granted what a supervisor states in a seminar. Lectures are perceived and vested with an authority which other British students may question because of earlier education. Such students may need to be enabled to adopt a critical stance, to whatever modes and voices they hear or read.

There may also be problems of different cultural interpretations which can lead to lower achievements by overseas students or those from cultural minorities residing in Britain. The cumulative effects – unless there is a supportive environment – can lead to further distancing between dominant and minority or students from other cultures. These may be exacerbated by inappropriate contributions to seminars or pieces of work submitted. Where tutors do not immediately and critically read students' work, students may continue to address issues, read and write research which only distantly relate to their dissertation.

ATTRIBUTES AND ATTRIBUTIONS OF THE DOCTORATE ITSELF

Patterns of organization and methods of research vary across different disciplines and faculties. It is possible that general guidelines may not be relevant to all situations, but the organization of an individual or collective ethos of enquiry may facilitate the capacity of students to optimize their research potential.

A community of scholars can develop if collaborative work leads to working collectively, engendering the development of critical audiences and providing articulate feedback (Eggleston and Delamont 1983: 63). Collaboration needs to be structured properly so that such activities are not competitive and can assist in establishing close working relations. The creation of a collective ethos which instils in all students, from dominant, minority, or overseas cultures, and between men and women, the desire to establish a common and shared understanding could be a useful and important starting point. There is also a need to provide for the development of study skills and English language skills for research purposes. Students can establish common sets of skills and shared meanings and help each other through different problems they come across. The tutors' role in this context is of paramount importance. The establishment of mechanisms during the early phase of students' work reduces problems for students and tutors at later points in the research. These mechanisms can include regular tutorials, where written work is submitted prior to the tutorial for discussions. Following tutorials a written report of points agreed upon, as well as future work to be undertaken, is often very useful. It can also form a record of the discussions as well as providing the student with a written record or guidance to work for the next tutorial.

Tutor feedback should be critical in nature to ensure that students can re-negotiate with specialist knowledge in their subject of research. Tutors ought to avoid flippant, personal, arrogant or ideologically laden comments which make it immensely difficult for students to continue to improve their work. Delicacy and balance are far more valuable to the student, especially since it is difficult for tutors to help their students to write well. For students with different first languages, writing in English has different cultural manifestations. They also face the complex task of establishing a relationship between the discourse and their discipline. Tutors have an important role in helping their students to understand the subject by opening gates rather than guarding them. Professor Brian Street's current research on the field of academic literacies for the Economic and Social Research Council may provide useful information on these issues.

An orientation programme at the beginning of doctoral work can help to ensure that students from patriarchal communities can relate to women tutors or fellow students without any problems. In the absence of such a collective ethos students and tutors can both confront awkward situations and misunderstandings. In general, however, doctoral students from overseas universities are imbued with egalitarian and modern values and tend to reject the patriarchal values of their families. It is more likely that British students who do not take the intellectual functions of universities seriously may hold on to the hierarchical and patriarchal values but may be better able to disguise them.

Racism in various forms is also likely to be experienced by students from non-dominant communities. Strong institutional policies and sanctions ought to regulate behaviours of all staff and students, whether in dealing with racism or sexism, to ensure that no student feels excluded or victimized. An institutional policy and named equal opportunity consultants in academic contexts ought to prove supportive of tutors and students.

Such institutional policies are far more important than the recommendations of writers like Phillips and Pugh (1994) who suggest that students ought to learn 'assertion techniques' (pp. 130–3). Such an approach leaves the onus of change on students when, in fact, it is institutions which need to change and facilitate diversity of staff and students. The intellectual dimension of 'assertiveness' would negate an openness of mind to the issues being researched, particularly if students also become academically arrogant. If anything supervisors and students both ought to develop an element of openness and humility in their interactions.

Academic institutions may construe certain types of difference as a deficit. For instance, students from other cultures may not previously have used English as used in specialist discourses within higher education but they may bring different conceptual frameworks, knowledge systems and, largely, a respect for learning and knowledge. If the institutions do not develop strategies to build on the diverse experiences then the notion of institutional change to accommodate diversity can only be negated. One of the mechanisms for ensuring that conceptual and theoretical constructs can be usefully built into the research frameworks students bring is to ensure that the language courses on offer enable students to extend their repertoires so that they can express complex ideas. The Institute of Education in London has pioneered quite elaborate ways of developing academic English and these may help in connecting students' knowledge with their expression in English. Supervisors and tutors in turn need to grasp the complexity involved in the transfer of conceptual frameworks from one linguistic system to another.

Some students from minority communities, like those in social policy and educational studies, who have taken the diploma route may have greater knowledge and facility for work within professional fields. However, students from these professional routes may not bring the scholarly orientation and knowledge of research methods to their doctoral work compared with those who have studied humanities, social sciences and sciences. Institutions which accept students from these backgrounds ought to consider providing adequate support so that these students can undertake doctoral research.

Those home students who have used the access routes and then undertake research in the new universities may be limited to undertaking only certain types of research in which supervisory competence is available. However, those students who move from new to old universities may bring a totally different understanding of research cultures which require development within the traditions of older universities. Such students may bring fresh insights. It is important that refining their research skills does not undermine the freshness or vivacity of their ideas.

The types of research undertaken also influence the levels of student competence and the nature of supervision students may require. For instance, those students who undertake fieldwork in their own home countries would require an expertise in fieldwork techniques, but they will be familiar with the culture of the country. This will obviously be an advantage. Students who register to undertake theoretical work with some component of fieldwork would obviously require higher levels of bi-cultural and bilingual competences. The supervision of such students also needs to have a different dynamic because students will be trying to make sense of complex literature and to construct an original argument for their own dissertation.

Students from different backgrounds and universities bring different strengths and weaknesses. Academic departments and tutors may need to acquire resources and expertise at an institutional level to deal with the complex levels of understanding and skills, as well as the lack of these that students bring with them. Tutors therefore require greater 'resources and capabilities so that the student, once accepted, does not fail for want of adequate tutorial support' (Eggleston and Delamont 1983: 62). Supervisory functions therefore enable an individual student from a disparate background to shift from being a relatively 'ill informed and undisciplined thinker to the author of a limited but definitive inquiry' (ibid.: 63).

The current institutional pressures on student completion rates and the pressure to complete the research in a prescribed time period because of the students' own financial constraints is seen by some as leading to students undertaking 'safe' projects for their research. As Phil Salmon suggests:

> a narrow time scale can mean a narrow scope. This narrowing would also, perhaps, inevitably be the effect of a doctoral programme which adds in a training element at the expense of original work.
>
> (Salmon 1992: 3)

Salmon raises the issue of generic taught courses as not necessarily being useful and suggests the need for research workshops which are 'firmly grounded in the needs and perceptions of students themselves' (ibid.: 4). Here, emphasis on the original contribution to knowledge arising out of the creative personal endeavour, which in turn leads to a transformative role for research, has particular significance for intercultural contexts. Students from 'other' cultures bringing 'other' knowledge systems can only engage in intellectually bold and imaginative research if there is institutional and tutorial support for it. Academic supervisors who function within narrow fields may not be able to assist in this process unless they themselves have an intellectually open mind, are well informed and are involved in their own professional, intellectual and academic development.

The British model of doctoral studies, where a student ploughs a lonely furrow, has greater potential for the student breaking new ground and uncovering new knowledge if they are well supervised. The North American model of taught courses only presents somewhat limited potential for developing students' exploration and imagination. Yet, paradoxically, the British model requires greater commitment on the part of staff and resources. The intellectual journey of the student requires personal confidence as well as academic and scientific expertise of the tutor to help define the exploration. The supportive function of tutorials, seminars and conferences is to ensure collaboration and co-operation and not competitiveness amongst students.

At this juncture there is a difference between Salmon, who relies on prolonged and intimate involvement without direction of the student, and researchers like Bourner and Barlow (1991) who recommend a more sustained tutor direction. Currently there is a danger in the total routinization and a bureaucratic direction for doctoral work which can sap the excitement and detract from the creative solitariness of doctoral work. Yet, in the intercultural context there is a need for genuine partnership between tutor and student to bring about a commitment to the field of enquiry. A median between the two positions may be more productive for students in intercultural contexts to optimize on their autonomy as well as to give them support.

Good tutors can engage with students' notions of deference for knowledge to develop greater levels of student autonomy through interaction with them. Supervision can also help in pre-empting blind alleys, and in retrieving certain situations before a student has gone down a counter-productive route.

The total routinization of doctoral work can also be further exacerbated if it is commodified and linked to the job market. Such doctoral work may not only undermine student autonomy and genuine commitment to the intrinsic value of education and research but also undermine the possible new directions within an intercultural context. The ways in which doctoral work can be transformed through intercultural directions would be aborted and retarded even further. This raises the fundamental question of what are the substantive inhibitors of an intercultural dimension in terms of content. This will be the next issue to be discussed in this chapter.

ATTRIBUTES OF KNOWLEDGE

Knowledge systems involve dual challenges because of Britain's colonial past and because it is involved in a narrowly defined process of European integration. On the one hand British universities endorse an Anglo-centric tradition in many domains of knowledge and on the other they assume a narrow European character for academic discourses. These hegemonic understandings are informed by the imperialism of Britain, as Edward Said writes:

> Without significant exception the universalizing discourses of modern Europe and the United States assume the silence, willing or otherwise, of the non-European world. There is incorporation; there is inclusion; there is direct rule; there is coercion. But there is only infrequently an acknowledgement that the colonized people should be heard from, their ideas known.
>
> (Said 1993: 58)

As a result of the imperial enterprise not only is Britain in the world but the world is in Britain. Ostensibly this has profound implications for the multilateral, bilateral and intercultural transfer of knowledge. The current reality obviously is that the transfer is primarily one way. Discourses from the colonized peripheries are still treated as being marginal in contemporary Britain.

Martin Bernal indicated how, in the eighteenth and nineteenth centuries, Europeans developed a historiography which denied the earlier understanding that the Greeks in the Classical and Hellenistic periods had acquired as a result of colonization and interaction between Egyptians, Phoenicians and Greeks (Bernal 1987). Part of the reason for this new historiography, was the rise of racism and anti-Semitism in Britain. Both Romantics and racists wanted to distance Greece from the Egyptians and Phoenicians and construct it as the pure childhood of Europe. This process was equally powerful in Scotland and England. The Scottish Enlightenment demonstrated its progressive elements and at the same time its profoundly xenophobic and narrowly nationalistic dimension. This complexity, which is reflected in some Scottish institutions, is partly a result of Scotland's role as a junior imperial partner. It was generally unacceptable, from such dominant perspectives, to concede that the British and Europeans might have gained any learning and understandings from the Africans or the Semites.

This historiographic shift has major implications for how British history is constructed, and particularly for how knowledge and linguistic systems from the civilizations construed as being inferior are excluded from the British academe. As Bernal states, the paradigm of 'progress' was used to put the Greeks to the fore and to cast aside the Egyptians, who were governed by priests. With the rise of slavery blacks were construed by British thinkers as uncivilized and consequently distanced from 'civilized' Britain. This exclusion has implications for what is taught about other civilizations and for how those who bring knowledge from other civilizations are perceived and construed.

The notion of a British culture connected with the Greek civilization but detached from other civilization systems is a mythical construction. Yet this is being perpetuated even now in the English context by the School Curriculum Assessment Authority, particularly by its chairman Dr N. Tate, who asserts the Greek origins of British culture but ignores the complex issues this poses. This type of perspective is subsequently reinforced within higher education. The contributions to knowledge in the ancient period from the Mediterranean region include Mesopotamian astronomy, the Egyptian calendar and Greek mathematics, enriched by the Arabs. As Samir Amin states:

> The opposition Greece = the West / Egypt, Mesopotamia, Persia = the East is itself a later artificial construct of Eurocentrism. For the boundary in the region separates the backward North African and European West from the advanced East; and the geographic unities constituting Europe, Africa and Asia have no importance on the level of the history of civilization, even if Eurocentrism in its reading of the past has projected onto the past the modern North-South line of demarcation passing through the Mediterranean.
>
> (Amin 1989: 24)

Amin argues that the Euro-Islamic medieval world ceased to exist during the Renaissance when Europe adopted the road towards capitalism:

> In Europe, civilization gradually wins over peoples of the North and East; to the South of the Mediterranean, Islamic culture gains ground in the Meghreb. Christianity and Islam are thus both heirs

of Hellenism and remain for this reason, twin siblings, even if they have been, at certain moments, relentless adversaries. It is probably only in the modern times – when Europe from Renaissance onward, takes off on the road towards capitalism that the Mediterranean boundary line forms between what will crystallize as the centre and periphery of the new worldwide and all-inclusive system.

(Amin 1989: 26)

The syncretisms of the Hellenistic period thus prepare the ground for Christianity and Islam and their universalistic messages. With the emergence of the Renaissance in Europe the dominance of metaphysics is broken and the material foundations of the capitalist world are laid. Scientific progress becomes manifest in the development of the forces of production in the context of a secularized society which becomes increasingly democratic.

The Renaissance is also a point of departure for the conquest of the world by Britain and Europe:

If the period of the Renaissance makes a qualitative break with the history of humanity, it is precisely because from that time on, Europeans become conscious of the idea of the conquest of the world by their civilization.

(Amin 1989: 72–3)

This is to a certain extent marked in 1492 by the mapping of the world, as well as the construction of a typology of different empires. As the relative strengths of different peoples and societies are tabulated, Eurocentrism is crystallized and it becomes a global project. This Europeanization of the globe bears within it an inherent de-universalization of knowledge, which developed for three hundred years from the Renaissance to the Enlightenment. It expressed itself as European, nationalist and secular with a worldwide scope. This dominant European culture had to arbitrarily and mythically construct its counterpart in 'the Other' and 'the Oriental'. (Gundara 1990). 'The other' and 'the oriental' are never thought of as quite civilized.

The Anglocentric dimension came into ascendency as Britain became part of the project of international dominance, and currently as it wants to form and dictate to a 'Fortress Europe'.

Critical to this is the construction of Greece as 'the pure childhood of Europe' and the severing of its link from its milieu in the Mediterranean, making it solely a part of Europe. Endemic to this is the racism of the North Europeans, in particular those who construct themselves as belonging to a superior and unified culture.

Knowledge systems constricted from such a foundation not only distort knowledge and its history but remain profoundly racist. The issues for intercultural education in Britain and Europe are not, therefore, as simplistic as critics of the North American context, like D'Souza, assert. His assertion that sound education is replaced by watered down knowledge of other cultures is not what is being suggested here (D'Souza 1992). This is so because the question of exclusion of substantive bodies of knowledge still remains unaddressed.

This legacy of distortion is based on the assumption that the Greek heritage predisposed Britain and Europe to rationality and, while Greece was the founder of rational philosophy, that the Orient is still locked into the metaphysical phase. As Amin asserts:

> The history of so-called Western thought and philosophy (which presupposes the existence of the other, diametrically opposed thoughts and philosophies, which is called Oriental) always begins with Greece. Emphasis is placed on the variety and conflicts of the philosophical schools, the development of thought free from religious constraints, humanism, and the triumph of reason – all without reference to the 'Orient' whose contribution to Hellenic thought is considered to be non-existent.
>
> (Amin 1989: 91)

This view of history assumes that the British took over Greek thought in the Renaissance and that this thought comes of age in modern philosophy. The period of two thousand years separating 'Greek antiquity from the European Renaissance are treated as a long and hazy period of transition' (ibid.). Amin's understanding of this issue resonates with Martin Bernal's research demonstrating the fabrication of ancient Greece.

For the British education system the challenge is to engage in a wide ranging establishment of connections with other cultures and civilizations which ought to be part of the fabric of contemporary understanding of its past which includes Greece, Egypt and the Near Eastern connections. The issue of Anglo-centrism is not simply an issue of prejudices and errors which heighten xenophobia and chauvinism. In discussing Eurocentrism Amin states that it has replaced:

rational explanations of history with partial pseudo-theories, patched together and even self contradictory at times. . . . The Eurocentric distortion that makes the dominant capitalist culture negates the universalist ambition on which that culture claims to be founded.

(Amin 1989: 104)

The Enlightenment came not as a universal phenomenon, despite attempts to learn from other cultures, but as a narrowly defined European response to the obscurantism of Christianity.

There are obvious contributions that the academic and educational systems can make in the context of democratic egalitarianism which is also a feature of British and European societies. Such theoretical issues should have implications for what constitutes the common curricula in British and European academe. Without such a curriculum individual groups are likely to demand separate education for their own nationality, religious or ethnic groups. The rise of ethnic, culturalist and fundamentalist nationalisms in Europe is a case in point, some of which have led to the abhorrent 'ethnic cleansing' and the breaking apart of nation states. At the core this remains a political issue but academic institutions do have a part to play in deconstructing this historiographic maze. The challenge therefore at postgraduate and doctoral work is to interculturalize the intellectual domain, something that poses a major challenge into the new millennium.

How are we to build conceptual and theoretical frameworks for higher degrees in different fields within British universities? These policies would obviously go some way towards correcting the biases in doctoral work which make access to all students contingent on their understanding of issues in the Anglo-centric mode. Such a framework would partly address issues of inequity and educational exclusion as they may have affected students from certain communities. There is a grave danger of students' demands for separate courses unless higher education institutions obviate the demands for separate ethnic studies for ethnic students. The development of separate curricula of recognition could particularly fragment doctoral studies into separate enclaves. Demands for an Islamo-centric or Afro-centric focus in higher education are being made to counteract Eurocentrism. Yet, the particularisms of different groups cannot be the logical conclusion of ending the Eurocentric focus. The intellectual process of dealing with Eurocentrism should, in fact, negate all forms of 'centrism' at higher education level. It should allow the emergence of a more inclusive basis of constructing curricula which is rigorously selective of human culture as a whole. Such proposals need to be presented to higher education institutions in ways which will ensure that they will be considered seriously.

Liberal education should seize this as a creative moment rather than set up barricades which would lead to reactive stances and postures. British universities need to liberate universalism and universal knowledge from the links of Anglo-centrism and Euro-centrism. Since universities demand a critical understanding of its doctoral students, they also ought to examine the rationale and intellectual basis of what is considered legitimate discourses within the academe.

The university systems continually confronted changes early in the nineteenth century. Curricular changes were introduced at Oxford from north of the border as a result of the Scottish Enlightenment. At the present time the canon is being questioned in many fields and domains of knowledge. The diverse contributions to these fields of knowledge ought to be examined with the aim of broadening the scope and range of what is taught to ensure that the best of literary and cultural knowledge, for instance, is available for all students at higher education institutions.

The field of art history illustrates the way in which Eurocentrism has either ignored or suppressed artistic contributions from certain civilizations. Yet, the contributions to the arts have been multifaceted and multifocal, both in the origins and in their development. In the eighteenth century the study of art history had an intercultural outlook. This was lost in the nineteenth and twentieth centuries and this territory needs to be reclaimed.

The dominance of Europe over other civilizations because of entrenched traditions and collecting became formalized as part of ethnology. Various ethnographic museums were established in the nineteenth century on both sides of the Atlantic. Their purpose was to allow the 'civilized man' to study the arts of those who were either savage or semi-civilized. To fit these arts into the canon of art appreciation a new category of 'primitive art' was created. The re-integration of various categories of the arts would now obviously raise critical issues for students in this field. Different questions in relation to the integration of other areas of knowledge and their aesthetics may themselves be researchable questions for newer doctoral students in the fields of the arts and literature.

Bernard Knox, the Emeritus Director of the Hellenic Centre at Harvard, stated:

> As for the multicultural curriculum that is the ideal of today's academic radicals, there can be no valid objection to the inclusion of new material that gives the student a wider view. But the new material will have to compete with the old, and if it is not up to the same high level it will sooner or later be rejected with disdain by the students themselves; only a totalitarian regime can enforce the continued study of second rate texts or outworn philosophies.
>
> (Knox 1993: 21)

In discussing an intercultural curriculum, there is no question of using second rate materials, either in the study of literatures or in art history. The question of understanding and developing an appropriate intercultural aesthetic is an issue of priority. Otherwise, students and supervisors will obviously reject texts, arts and artifacts as unfamiliar or second rate.

Many students from non-European communities assume that the sciences, technologies and mathematics as disciplines are essentially part of a western or European tradition. In many cases their interest or knowledge in subjects which are viewed as being alien leads to levels of performance which do not match their capacities. British scholarship has pioneered many aspects of the histories of ideas (Bernal 1956: Needham 1981) which ought to inform doctoral research of students in many disciplines. Many tutors remain unaware of developing their specializations to optimize the intellectual potentials of all their students, especially those from 'other' cultures and traditions.

Some academics and intellectuals in higher education stereotype any suggestion of staff development to broaden their specialization as political correctness, imported from across the Atlantic. However, issues being raised here do suggest basic questions about what is seen to constitute the corpus of legitimate knowledge at doctoral level. Suggestions of broadening the bases of knowledge and skills are commensurate with the intellectual role and functions of universities and not a demand for special consideration. A broad curriculum is an entitlement for all students whatever their background. Universities should ensure that all doctoral students but especially those from 'other' backgrounds can gain the most out of their research studies. The development and the role of integrated curriculum in building common and shared reference points is a legitimate concern.

British universities seeking to provide for students at an international level need to make a programmatic effort to develop a coherent curriculum. Such developments necessitate the mobilization of teaching and research functions to enable universities to revitalize higher education through institutional policies and practice. Individual academics have a contribution to make in this effort to enable them to maintain high standards and enable the supervision of doctoral students to be of high quality.

The question is whether these policies and initiatives would impair or impinge on the autonomy of academics in universities. The contention of this chapter is that a universally derived curriculum which is more intercultural would enhance the academic autonomy of staff and not detract from it. The issue here is not one of tackling the attitudes or the personal and private belief systems of academics. The question is basically about the public role of academics as professional members of public institutions, where they have wide ranging obligations to develop an unbiased access to knowledge for themselves and their students (D'Souza 1992).

A number of scholars have undertaken research into the mutual borrowings between South Asia and Europe, particularly in science and technology (Lach 1977). The cross-fertilization of scientific and mathematical ideas between China, South Asia, Arabia and Europe is an important example of developing intercultural conceptual and theoretical frameworks in the sciences. Such developments obviously require complex responses from science and technology faculties. Specialist researchers may need to evaluate their subjects in relation to knowledge from other civilizations and to consider joint or interdisciplinary supervision of students. If knowledge from more than one domain can contribute to developing doctoral research, then supervisory functions might be optimized.

CONCLUSIONS

This chapter has dealt with aspects of interculturalism as they impinge on doctoral studies in Britain. The chapter has raised issues about attributes and attributions of students, doctoral programmes and the curriculum. Issues have been raised in an introductory manner partly because there is very little substantive analysis of the way in which exclusivities and xenophobia are operationalized within doctoral programmes. North American research in the field is more extensive but has little direct relevance because of the

qualitative differences between British and American doctoral programmes.

The very low take-up of doctoral studies from certain sections of
the British and overseas student body is exacerbated by higher costs
of doctoral studies. Positive measures are needed to ensure that the
higher reaches of the academe do not become a preserve of those
who can afford it.

Multicultural student bodies, intercultural practices and the curriculum present new challenges to doctoral studies. The older universities with a longer tradition of research ought to become more
flexible in refining their skills, knowledge and practices. This would
allow them to raise academic standards for doctoral research with a
diverse body of students and a more universalized basis of knowledge. It is, however, the newer universities which may be more open
to these ideas and able to acquire the skills to help students from
different backgrounds and thus reap the rewards of these necessary
changes into the next millennium.

NOTES

1 The terms 'ethnic', 'minority' and 'black' are used advisedly in this
   chapter. There are few terms which academics agree upon since each of
   these terms raises problems among different constituencies of the
   academic community working in this field.
2 I would like to thank Dr Phil Salmon, Sarah Jones and Alice Henfield
   for their help.

REFERENCES

Amin, S. (1989) *Eurocentrism*, London: Zed Books.

Bernal, J.D. (1956) *Science and History*, New York: Hawthorn Books.

Bernal, M. (1987) *Black Athena: The Afroasiatic Roots of Classical
Civilisation*, London: Free Association Press.

Bourner, T. and Barlow, J. (1991) *Part-time Students and Their Experience
of Higher Education*, Buckingham: Open University Press.

D'Souza, D. (1992) *Illiterate Education: The Politics of Race and Sex on
Campus*, New York: Vintage Books.

Eggleston, J. and Delamont, S. (1983) *Supervision of Students for Research
Degrees*, BERA.

Gundara, J. (1990) 'Social Diversities and Issues of the Other', *Oxford
Review of Education*, Vol. 16, No. 1.

Knox, B. (1993) *The Oldest Dead White European Males*, New York: W.N.
Norton.

Lach, D.F. (1977) *Asia in the Making of Europe*, Vol. 11, Chicago: University of Chicago Press.

Needham, J. (1981) *Science in Traditional China: A Comparative Perspective*, Hong Kong: Chinese University Press.

Phillips, F.M. and Pugh, D.S. (1994) *How to get a PhD*, Buckingham: Open University Press.

Said, E. (1993) *Culture and Imperialism*, London: Chatto and Windus.

Salmon. P. (1992) *Achieving a PhD: On Student Experience*, Stoke-on-Trent: Trentham.

Chapter 9

Gender issues in doctoral studies[1]

Diana Leonard

The proportion of women students has been steadily increasing in most western countries for many years and they now comprise half of all undergraduate and one-third of postgraduate research students in Australia, Britain and the USA. But differences between men and women are ignored in debates about higher education planning, with the consequence that, even when changes are introduced, higher education (HE) remains geared to men's rather than women's needs. So, although many women are currently doing quite well, they are doing so against the odds.

In the UK, for instance, all the recent debates about the desirable form for the PhD ignore gender issues. The Economic and Social Research Council produced the key Winfield Report in 1987 because of its concern with the numbers who started work on a thesis but who failed to complete it; the 'excessive' time taken to complete by many of those who did finish; the issue of whether or not candidates got an adequate training in methodology; and whether or not the PhD qualification was relevant to the needs of many employers. But, as Sara Delamont pithily commented, 'an all-male committee consulted male experts to produce a report focused on male graduate students' (Delamont 1989: 52). As a consequence, the concrete changes introduced, which include improving the support for students provided by universities, the introduction or systematizing of a taught research training programme and treating completion after more than four years as 'late' completion, have all been set up assuming (and hence best fitting) full-time, geographically mobile, trainee social 'scientists'. Hence they present difficulties for all those who do not fit this profile because of their domestic commitments, residence, career profile or discipline. And hence they impact differentially on (different groups of) men and women, who have, overall, differing family responsibilities, possibilities for geographical mobility, academic interests, etc.

Not only was the Winfield Report itself biased, so was the research conducted for it (e.g. Young, Fogarty and McRae 1987) and, similarly, the subsequent ESRC 'Research into Training' programme set up to look at 'the UK's social science research training, academic community, labour market prospects and individual careers'. (For interesting insights on this, see Acker 1994: 61ff.) This programme funded nine projects from 1988–91, but the first collection of papers from a dissemination conference in 1992 (Burgess 1994) contained not one focused on gender; and most do not comment at all on possible differences between men and women, or between different sorts of men and women (i.e. variations by race, age, class background, etc.). These debates have also, by and large, ignored the

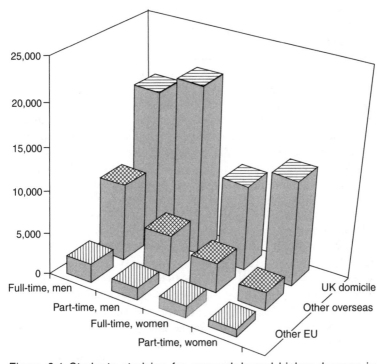

Figure 9.1 Students studying for research-based higher degrees in the UK in 1994–5, by sex and domicile (N=86,961)
Source: HESA 1996, Tables 1c and 1g

existence (and specific needs) of the large numbers of overseas and European Union students who are currently studying for research-based higher degrees in the UK (see Figure 9.1).

FEMINIST CONCERNS

While mainstream debates on higher education continue to ignore gender, the imbalance between men and women students caused grave concern to the emergent women's movements in western countries in the early 1970s. At that time, national surveys showed men to comprise 84 per cent of successful doctoral students in the US (Astin and Malik 1994: 187) and 85 per cent in the UK in 1972 (Rudd in association with Simpson 1975), and 86 per cent in Australia in 1977 (Allen 1994: 15). The low proportion of women PhDs bothered feminists both because it was a restriction on women's entry to and advancement within a particular profession, academia; and, more importantly, because universities were seen as privileged centres for the production and validation of knowledge. To change views on women it was seen as essential to change the knowledge production and validation processes; i.e. to get more research done on, by and for women. (For an early classic statement of this point see Dorothy Smith (1978).)

Individual women therefore produced 'consciousness raising' accounts of their own experiences of higher education, and studies were made of particular universities to influence internal policy-making and practice. In addition, more systematic national surveys and detailed ethnographic studies were produced in the US, Canada and Australia from the 1970s onwards. While most such work has focused on undergraduates and on faculty, there *is* now a reasonable body of research specifically on gender and graduate studies, and most mainstream studies of higher education in North America have routinely analysed by sex since the 1960s (see for example for the US: Astin 1969; Centra 1974; Feldman 1974; Holmstrom and Holmstrom 1974; Katz and Hartnett 1976; Vartuli 1982; Sandler and Hall 1986; for Canada: Filteau 1989; Caplan 1994; and for Australia: Powles 1986; Moses 1990, 1992; Conrad 1994).

In Britain, however, despite similar participation rates, relatively little attention has been given to women in research on higher education, and there is a minimal amount of work on gender and doctoral studies (though see Blackstone 1975; Rendel 1975; Wood-hall 1975; Taylorson 1980, 1984; Scott and Porter 1983; and

Goldsmith and Shawcross 1985). Most mainstream work here has continued to pretend that there are no, or only minor, gender differences among students (as it has similarly ignored racial and ethnic differences, age differences, overseas students' situations, disabled students, etc). Many writers do not even get to the first base of providing breakdowns by sex in their tables and some continue to produce some very 'retro' attitudes as they slide into talking about 'students and their wives'. The same is also true of most 'self-help' books for PhD students and those writing dissertations generally, though there are special sections on women in a few (e.g. Phillips and Pugh 1994). There are also books and sections addressed to overseas students, but not so far as I know to black research students.

However, even in the best cases, texts do not address the specific concerns of those who are *both* women *and* from overseas, even though the first (and so far only) study to look at women students from the poorer countries of the world studying in the UK, carried out by the World University Service (WUS) in 1983 (Goldsmith and Shawcross 1985), shows that the issues facing such students are not simple additions of the problems identified for 'women' (i.e. home women) and 'overseas' (i.e. overseas men), but rather have their own specific features. The WUS study also obtained a breakdown of national statistics by country of origin which showed that the poorest countries had the fewest women relative to men studying in the UK – though the numbers of women were also low from OPEC and Middle Eastern countries. Its interviews with students showed that most overseas women students (like many home women students) are from upper- or upper-middle-class backgrounds (Goldsmith and Shawcross 1985; see also Unterhalter and Maxey 1995). Not only gender and national but also social economic background intersect and all need to be taken into account in understanding and changing 'student' experiences.

There is thus now a gender literature (and also to a lesser extent an overseas, part-timers, and 'race', etc. literature) on students in higher education, including research students (though the literature on part-timers and on race in the UK is mainly concerned with continuing, adult and further education, and access to HE, not with graduate students; while the US literature, which does cover race and graduate students, does not translate easily to the UK context because of the different nature of the PhD and also because of different patterns of class and ethnicity and the existence of historically black colleges). Against which there is a parallel, mainstream literature which deals with 'ungendered' research students – who are implicitly male, young and from the home country. This reconstructs the advantages of the normative group by treating everyone who is not male etc. as different or deviant and as having (or rather as being) a problem. And the situation of the multiple not young white middle-class males is hidden.

REASONS FOR DOING A PhD

In the current debates, the dominant – government – discourse concerns the need to make the PhD a training for high quality generic researchers (i.e. to make sure young students become skilled in choosing and using appropriate methods) and relevant to the needs of employment and the nation's economic growth and competitiveness. The PhD is apprenticeship work which should be completed promptly.

Against this, a debate is finally being more systematically mounted by those who take an 'educational' stance: who say a PhD is about personal development, intellectual growth and satisfaction; and that unlike a PhD in science or engineering, a social science or humanities thesis is expected to produce *important* original work – and that this takes time.

While individual men and women may have a variety of reasons for embarking on the long process of acquiring a doctorate, some of which are vocational, most include a desire for intellectual challenge and an intrinsic interest in research. This is especially true of those who want to do research in the social sciences and humanities and of those who return to study after a period of employment. Hence it is true of more women research students than men, since more women are in these fields and follow this life path. Ingrid Moses (1990), on the basis of work in Australia, stresses that rather than undertaking research directly after their first degree, as a 'closed loop' continuous planned educational career, women often start to do a PhD after a period of employment (and, she says, most have had several jobs rather than a period out of the labour market caring for children) as part of a personal development progression. They express this as undertaking a PhD because of 'a need for a change', to counter job burnout, or as 'taking charge of one's life' and/or prioritizing their own self-development (see also Vartuli 1982: 22 on the US).

Another reason women often come late to their PhDs is tied to a phenomenon widely noted in the literature on gender and education:

that girls and women tend to think that *if* they are good enough, someone will notice and encourage them to proceed. But with PhDs, as elsewhere in life, this is not true, and certainly not true for women. Women are *less* likely to be encouraged by their teachers than men (Moses 1994; Salmon 1992). Individuals have to put themselves forward and be confident – and women are trained to be self-effacing and diffident. Women are also less likely to get first class degrees (i.e. the work they do is less likely to be perceived as exceptional) and they do not get the same opportunities to interact with women professionals as men do with men professionals (i.e. they are less likely to understand academic processes well and they are less likely to be seen to have potential). Where faculty do recommend women to do postgraduate work, the women are likely to be under thirty. Older women get their support and encouragement mainly from family and friends; and they may initially hesitate to do postgraduate work because they do not perceive that such study will make a difference to their career prospects.

TIME AND MONEY

Whatever the motivations for wanting a PhD, the central problems facing any potential suitably qualified student are having or finding the time and money to undertake the work – and not only time for the project and required courses, but also to attend conferences and seminars and other aspects of the research culture – and then finding a supervisor.

As noted above, the training perspective has reinforced the idea that doctoral students should be able to complete quickly (so able to live on a grant and work full-time on the research, i.e. without a job and with no major domestic responsibilities) and geographically mobile (able to go and live in an appropriate place). This presents invidious choices to older students, women students and above all overseas students. Overseas women students may be forced to choose between marriage and higher education (and women from the poorest countries are more likely to marry earlier than women from richer ones) or between studying overseas and remaining with their family and young children.

Financial or other constraints may force many male students to make this difficult choice also. But it is a harder choice for women to make, given the particular expectation and social pressure on women to remain with their families.

(Goldsmith and Shawcross 1985: 22)

It is also a harder choice for women – and this may hit home students too if research training becomes concentrated in a relatively small number of élite universities so that study comes to require a move of house – because wives are more likely to accompany husbands than vice versa. This gets hidden at present by silences in the existing literature. Thus we are told by one study that

> A large proportion of the [overseas] students surveyed were married and had families, and many of them wished to have their partners and families accompany them to Britain, especially research students who would be resident for more than one year. However, both universities [Nottingham and Loughborough] advised against this due to a lack of suitable accommodation. . . . Some male students found they had difficulty in catering for themselves and had sent for their families so that their wives could undertake time-consuming domestic chores. [However] Wives were lonely and isolated, often with no English and with young children obstructing the opportunity to learn, [so] male students found themselves solely responsible for shopping, overseeing schooling, rent arrangements, transport, medical matters and similar, all interfering with studies.
>
> (Lewins 1990: 92–3)

But the authors say nothing comparable about women students and their husbands and children – or about how women fare alone.

Women research students may also encounter specific problems with grants – nearly half of overseas students have a scholarship or grant of some kind from their government or British funds, and these may not pay allowances for (women's) dependents nor cover payment for childcare. In addition, women students used to have different legal rights in terms of bringing in their dependents:

> a man [under immigration restrictions] who is in Britain to study can be accompanied by his wife and children under 18, but because women are not classified as 'head of household', the equivalent right has never been afforded to female students or female work-permit holders.
>
> (Goldsmith and Shawcross 1985: 6)

Some of this has now been taken on board by funders – e.g. by Commonwealth institutions and the European Union – who wish to increase the numbers of women they support. They now require women to be among those nominated, although the tendency to offer postgraduate scholarships in the sciences, technology and engineering, agriculture, veterinary, forestry and other 'development' subjects and to select candidates from among the employees of institutes and government administrations still militates against women. And there is still a lack of family accommodation and childcare available for students in British universities.

Moses in particular stresses that mature women home students too really need to have scholarships or study leave from their employment so that they can study full-time, and to have money in these grants for the care of children under 12 years of age, since, she says, graduate study is otherwise difficult if not impossible. It is very hard indeed to combine part-time work, part-time care for a family, part-time study and part-time cultivation of intellectual networks. Currently, however, women home students are actually *less* likely to get grants than men – not, according to Moses, because of direct discrimination in selection by awarding bodies, but again because most women want to do PhDs in the social sciences and humanities where there is less state or commercial funding, and because fewer have first class degrees than men (Moses 1990: 35). Women certainly need to have grants to at least pay their fees, because (as has been shown by research in the sociology of the family, see e.g. Pahl 1989), they do not have the same rights to call upon 'family' money for their 'personal' spending as do men.

Of course many women undertaking PhDs are childfree and not yet caring for the elderly, and many do not have men partners. But that does not mean that gender does not affect their situation. Both men and women students experience enormous changes in their first year of graduate study if they give up a well-paid job; and both sexes are lonely if they move home, especially on their own. But income and job status are particularly important to women, whose worth and time is differentially evaluated from (that is to say, it is valued less than) that of men. For instance, single women are seen as having all the time in the world and as being selfish if they don't spend it helping others. Some of my young women students have found themselves required to devote weeks to taking care of relatives who have come on holiday or to hospitals in London. Lesbian students and minority ethnic or black students who move out of big cities to campus universities may find themselves extremely isolated away from a sizeable, visible community. Moreover, men and women have different patterns of sociability, and sport and public spaces are both more available to men.

The culture gap between Britons and overseas students is again something that women may experience with greater severity than men. Many of the environments in which British students relax may be inhospitable to overseas women. A Mauritian student complained: 'Men can go to bars, but I have been brought up not to drink and smoke.'

(Goldsmith and Shawcross 1985: 25)

In other words, though highly variable, women's financial, time and locality contraints are systematically different from men's. Moreover, women have in common that both they and their supervisors are more likely to focus on their non-academic lives when talking about 'problems' or difficulties with their research (Scott and Porter 1983). This does not mean that their 'private' lives are actually more problematic for their progress, merely that they are seen to be.

There is, however, little difference between men and women doctoral students in their career motivation – they are equally dedicated scholars. Women may be slightly less likely to be vocationally oriented, less likely to have drifted in to doing a PhD, and less likely to be centrally concerned with salary and promotion, but they do aspire equally with men to high status, currently male-dominated, careers.

Men and women have in common too that, if they are to stick with their course of study, they have to fit their research into other aspects of their lives. Both sexes and both full- and part-timers need to consult family and friends before undertaking the degree because it will substantially affect relationships and other commitments for somewhere between four and ten years.

Everyone has to find within themselves ways of working on their own piece of research which both fit with the rest of their lives and – at least at times – bring about a sense of progress. All this is very difficult. The creative process is itself notoriously capricious. Most PhD students, additionally, have both work and family or domestic responsibilities, leaving only limited time and energies available for research. In the case of many women students in particular, there are often inner barriers against a confident claim to spend time on their personal work. Yet given that, for most students, their PhD project represents their first experience of independent research. It is at this stage that a personally viable mode of work needs to be discovered.

(Salmon, 1992: 22)

FINDING A SUPERVISOR AND A UNIVERSITY

The relationship between student and supervisor has had a lot of attention given to it by both those stressing the training and those stressing the educational aspects of the PhD. For the former, the relationship with the supervisor has been seen as the main cause of low completion rates which the university itself can tackle (by better monitoring of student progress and staff development programmes for supervisors). For those stressing education, the importance of the relationship with the supervisor to the student's personal development puts it 'at the heart of doctoral work'. Salmon describes agreeing to a supervisory relationship as an agreement to work in long-term close collaboration: to embark on a journey together (Salmon 1992: 21). The self-help literature also talks a lot about handling one's supervisor. But what the focus on the one-to-oneness of the relationship perhaps overlooks is that it is this exclusiveness which is often part of the trouble. It is important also to pay attention to the context within which it is located.

The discipline is a primary source of identity in postgraduate studies and provides the framework for the research; and there are major differences in the experiences of women by discipline, as Moses makes clear. There are also departmental variations within disciplines – some departments are more prestigious than others, and a mark of prestige can be a chilly climate for women. For instance it used to be UC Berkeley sociology department's proud boast that it had never appointed a woman member of staff – the results can be read in the accounts of the first women who gained their doctorates there (see Orlans 1994). There are also differences in departments' theoretical allegiances and preferred types of methodology – some are more and some less woman/feminist friendly. And another source of difference is in the proportion of women students and the absolute numbers of research students in a given department. Even though a high proportion of women students does not mean women will dominate seminars or even that they will get an equal share of resources (see Thomas 1990), there are still differences in the experience of being in a very small or in a moderate-sized minority; and where there is a sizeable number of research students in a department and a high proportion of women, it is much easier to establish academic peer groups and networks which can improve women's freedom of interaction and participation. It certainly helps to avoid the terrible visibility/invisibility of someone's being, for example, the *only* overseas or black woman student. In such situations individuals find they constantly stand out but equally their needs are never central to the main agenda.

There has also been a certain amount of discussion of whether or not it is generally helpful to women students to have a woman supervisor (recognizing this will not always be possible, since most supervisors are men and many students are women in the social sciences and humanities: Taylorson 1984; Acker 1992). It certainly cannot be just any woman, since not all women have empathy with women students and some are downright hostile, but in general women supervisors, or if not supervisors then other women staff, are helpful to women students.

This does not mean that there needs to be *a* women on the staff to provide a 'role model' (though this is how it often gets expressed when appointments are being considered – and conversely it is said that 'we don't need another woman' when there are already one or two). Rather, women students need a range of women staff around; and women staff need to have time available to offer help, both when there is blatant misogyny and, more routinely, because western women students feel easier talking about personal problems to a woman, and women from certain cultures feel comfortable talking only to women, even about their work. (This does not imply that men who are not comfortable being taught by a woman should be allowed to express such views and assigned to a male supervisor. Liberals may argue the same rules should apply to both sexes, but radical analysis requires differential treatment for dominated and dominant groups.) Women staff, especially senior women staff and professors, are also more likely to be skilled in supporting topics low in the pecking order of importance in the discipline, which includes many areas popular with women, and they are used to handling issues of 'objectivity' versus 'commitment' in research and arguing for the legitimacy of particular (feminist) theoretical frameworks and methodologies.

It is here perhaps salutory to pause and consider why supervisors take on students. As Hockey and colleagues note (Hockey 1991), it is often an academic's way of doing surrogate research – of keeping on top of the field, researching an area of potential interest, getting specific intellectual stimulation and new insights, establishing a new academic network, and joint publications – and having fun.

Those students interested in doing research on gender or women should therefore be warned that many men (and some women) academics have not read the literature in this field and, even though they may express an interest, they will not be able to help a student towards the necessary overturning of sexist paradigms to ask important research questions. (They will probably send the student off 'to talk to a feminist they know', far too late in the day for it to be helpful to the research project!) Rather academics hope that through working with a student they themselves will learn. Most have no notion of what has been achieved (theoretically, methodologically and empirically) by feminist researchers – note the point made earlier about the parallel strands of work on higher education itself and specialists producing national reports not knowing the literature 'on women' (see Allen and Leonard 1996). So if someone wants to do research on gender, or if the field they are interested in has a possible gender dimension, they should make sure they get a specialist as co-supervisor, or at the least they should attend a good related course on women's studies in their university. Otherwise they simply will not know what they are missing until it is too late – and 'what they are missing' is both scholarly insight into their material and the intellectual excitement and sense of solidarity that exists in this rapidly growing field.

Getting a feminist supervisor is not always easy, however, since feminist academics are thin on the ground and black feminists an endangered species. Moreover, even though women academics are often attracted to teaching and prepared to take on quite heavy loads, this makes it difficult for them to do research and publish – especially since extra pastoral work certainly also makes its way to their door. They are therefore nowadays under pressure and often unable to bridge the gap between available resources and legitimate student demands (Skeggs 1995).

Whatever else they may or may not be able to do for their students, a supervisor of either sex should be a good sponsor (see Williams, Blackstone and Metcalfe 1974):

> Two important ingredients of a successful graduate career mentioned in the American literature . . . are a close relationship

with an academic sponsor and integration with a student reference group. These provide the essential professional socialization and foster the development of the appropriate self-image. However . . . the gender of the graduate student will affect the likelihood of their receiving sponsorship from academic staff, so that male students have a better chance of being sponsored than females. Gender will also be one of the factors influencing membership of student peer groups. Women may be less likely than men to be included in those informal learning situations that arise outside the research situation or the formal university seminar . . . coffee breaks, lunch or an evening drink.

(Taylorson 1984: 147–9)

However, when women are sponsored and included, it may be on different terms and conditions from men, and the 'fun' in relations between supervisors or other staff members and students may include sexual and/or romantic attachments. The fact that most supervisors are men and most such relationships heterosexual means that the students involved are usually women. Similar comments can be made, however, about same-sex relationships and women staff's involvement with men students – though the way sexual dynamics are constructed in our society does affect the power balances in these atypical cases (see Bacchi 1992, 1994). These are seductive relationships because research students are vulnerable and see themselves as getting support from someone they wish to please, who understands their goals and ambitions, shares the excitement of intellectual endeavour, has access to helpful inside information, and will increase their chances of success. But just as the medical profession and psychologists have warned members against this type of intimacy and discussed its being both unethical and detrimental to the treatment process, so there are arguments against amorous relationships between teachers and students.

Within weeks of the [professional training] course starting X had commenced an affair with one of the students in the groups. She was highly flattered by his attention and made no secret of the relationship. It, however, made it very uncomfortable for the rest of us who were aware that in all probability our comments about the course as well as our dissatisfaction about the poor teaching of that lecturer were being carried back to him. The relationship continued until the end of the year when he selected a new student from the incoming first year. The student in our group felt both humiliated and bitter. She never really had much to do with the rest of us after that and became a very irregular attender.

(Carter and Jeffs 1992: 454)

To warn against such relationships is not to be a killjoy who cannot recognize that knowledge is sexy (cf. Mintz 1967; Gallop 1993 quoted Bacchi 1994: 55), nor to infantalize students and make women into victims by denying them the opportunity, or saying they are unable, to make decisions about how they live their lives (Roiphe 1993). On the contrary, it involves accepting Diane Purkiss's argument that pedagogy and seduction have been semiotically intertwined since Plato (Purkiss 1994), and that seduction is possibly more of a problem where there is not a huge age difference, i.e. when the woman is older. (Eighteen-year-old students are part of a peer group which can provide a strong defence.) Rather it is an abuse of power, overwhelmingly between male academics and female students, and the fact that it happens – that it is allowed to happen, because it could be treated as breach of professional conduct (as unethical and reprehensible for an academic to have a sexual, or indeed a family or financial relationship with any student under his or her supervision or whose work he will be marking), as has been recommended in policies produced by the Federation of Australian Staff Associations (1989), the Canadian Association of University Teachers (1990) and the British Association of University Teachers (1993) – means that women students and staff have constantly to be circumspect in their dealings with male staff.

When a male student goes for a drink with his male supervisor he is perceived as an ambitious and sociable person; but when a female student is in the same situation she is in danger of being perceived as flirtatious or even as already being 'involved' with her supervisor.

(Phillips and Pugh 1994: 121–2)

Phillips and Pugh comment that 'Innocent and perfectly acceptable social contact becomes tainted with gossip and innuendo'; but it is rather that an always problematic, unequal relationship (between tutor and student and between men and women) is used to confirm women in their place both within the individual relationship and within the wider public domain. Hence it is detrimental to the learning of the students involved and to all others (especially all women) in the same department, and involves a much wider debate about the part played by heterosexuality in gender relations (and vice versa) and about what constitutes consent in unequal relationships.

Certainly women students should be wary of certain male members of staff who can only be described as predatory. They run through every new woman graduate and staff member who comes onto campus. The women involved find themselves humiliated when their seduction becomes public knowledge. A 1993 survey of 500 postgraduate and trainee psychologists – most of them women – found that nearly half had had intimate relationships with their supervisors which they subsequently regretted (Glaser and Thorpe 1986). (The men concerned are, however, vituperative if they hear warnings about them are being given to students by their colleagues – see on.) Women considering such a relationship should also know for just how long any success they may have will be at least partly attributed to the relationship. (Ten years on people will still say 'She only got through her *viva* because she was sleeping with Y'.) Also that lovers can make you unemployable in their own university; and that even if the relationship should end in marriage, this is not necessarily a 'positive supportive consequence' for the women involved (*pace* Williams 1982: 91), but rather the entry into a different form of exploitative relationship. (See Delphy and Leonard (1992), especially chapter 9, for information on how male academics use their wives' labour.)

This topic also raises the issue of whether or not there are more general problems in *all* close staff friendships with students. Some have argued this is favouritism because such students are given extra time and advice (see Bacchi 1994: 57, fn. 10; and papers in Cahn 1990). The professoriate has 'diffuse power' and controls access to future advancement by recommendation and providing research and teaching opportunities for students – and this is indeed a way in which men students are routinely given preference by the largely male faculty. Since such relationships do exist, however, Moses emphasises how important mentors and sponsors of either sex are for a woman; but she also comments on the vicious circle which exists because of the serious shortage of same-sex mentors, especially for minority ethnic women.

The significance of gender in inter-relations with the supervisor is, however, not noted in any of the self-help books. Moses, quoting studies of Sydney and Melbourne Universities as well as her own national study in Australia, says that the informal nature of supervision may deny women the support they particularly need. Most women express satisfaction with their supervisor (though they are less satisfied than men), but women, especially older women, not only generally miss out on 'the beneficial aspects of regular and frequent interaction with other academic staff in the department', they also do not get as much access to or help from their own supervisor(s) as men (Moses 1990: 32–5). Moreover, men and women often do not understand each other's conversational styles, and men supervisors seem particularly to misunderstand – or perhaps it is the tension of the one-to-one situation that heightens – women students' silences and their use of narratives and personal experience which men see as inappropriate (Lewis 1993; Conrad 1994; Gold 1995).

KEEPING GOING

There is no doubt that doing a PhD is a stressful experience, no less so (indeed precisely) because it is in many ways a privileged situation. It is especially stressful in the social sciences and humanities, where producing a thesis takes longer and the work is less structured and can be very isolating. Vartuli's edited collection on *The PhD Experience: a woman's point of view* has a whole chapter on stress – concentrating especially on the first year and the comprehensive exams (in the US), but looking also at more general issues of status, money, the need to build a new support system, and the physical effects of changed patterns of diet, recreation and socialization (Vartuli 1982). In relation to housing, it is important to have a space where you can leave work undisturbed and come back to it later – which many women do not have, especially if sharing a house with family members. (The Brontë sisters may have written great novels, but it was their brother who had the study. The women in the family had to clear their books off the table for every meal.)

For both men and women, the first year can produce a loss of their sense of balance in life. Overseas students experience the same unease in their first six months as home students, but for them this is exacerbated by the disorientation of studying in another environment (Channell 1990). The difficulties of life in Britain include the cost and discomfort of accommodation (and women may not be used to looking for this for themselves), cold weather, lack of provision for dietary religious and cultural differences, and, frequently, a sense of social isolation (Goldsmith and Shawcross 1985). To this can be added issues of racism, sexism and homophobia. So, for example, walking home in the dark from the library may be as unsafe for overseas men as it is for all women, since young men experience more violence than older men in western society, and foreigners, racial minorities and gay men are especially likely to be picked upon. However, women are more likely to *feel* fear and to constrain their movements accordingly. They (or their family and male compatriots) are more likely to be concerned about them working late at night in computing rooms or when interviewing in people's homes.

Added to this, and increasing as time goes on, many women have problems of chronic lack of confidence, despite the good academic results they have achieved and/or the professional expertise they have displayed in their jobs before undertaking dotoral studies. Many go on questioning whether they can manage a PhD and whether it is worth its personal and professional costs throughout the time they are working on it – though they may feel they have to be circumspect in revealing these uncertainties and their distress to male faculty because they are worried people will 'find out' they 'got in by mistake' (see e.g., from the substantial literature on this topic: Vartuli 1982; Sandler and Hall 1986; Caplan 1994).

This is not all in women's heads. Caplan in particular stresses how women are made to feel uncomfortable in academia, to doubt their abilities, to become unproductive and to feel they don't belong, so they leave. Universities are said to prize rationality and objectivity and to be meritocratic: but it is not just merit but a lot of other things – including sponsorship and male bonding – that determines who is successful. Academia is also supposedly involved in a co-operative search for knowledge, with rewards for honesty and collaboration, but it is in fact often duplicitous, exploitative and fiercely competive, and it does not reward – indeed it sometimes does not even allow – collaboration, as is evident in the PhD itself. Moreover, as is well attested experimentally, women's work is routinely less well evaluated (because of what it is about, how it is done, and/or straight- forwardly because it has a woman's name on it); and while male success is attributed to solid abilities, women's is often said to be due to luck or hard work. Women who are scholarly and ambitious are hardfaced; women who are not should not be keeping a deserving man out of a job.

This 'chilly climate' for women can also involve being told directly that they are not wanted (especially if they are black, lesbian, middle aged or feminist) via a variety of forms of hostile comments and behaviour. Sexual harassment was originally defined as a demand for sexual contact from someone with power, backed by threats of reprisals; but it has commonly been expanded to cover the creation of a generally discomforting work environment. This can involve touching, staring, comments, jokes, insults, sneers, ignoring women or picking on them, and displaying material which makes women feel embarassed – things which never let women forget they are women, which emphasize their subordinate position, which give men a buzz by affirming they are not women, and which take up women's time and energy in coping with them. Since this hostility is a response to threats to male supremacy, it is used more against higher status women. Women research students will be used to dealing with sexist behaviour in general, but they will probably find the level increases as they move from master's to doctoral studies.

It is difficult to handle this, because just calling behaviour 'sexual harassment' is often treated as though it were a form of violence against men: an intrusion on their rights. Caroline Ramazanoglu suggests men's opposition is due to their freedoms being restricted and because it is no longer clear what they can and cannot do (Ramazanoglu 1987) – so it is women's complaints which are seen as the problem – and also because harassment grades into the general maleness and pervasive sexism of the university and the culture. (See the way in which women having a drink with their supervisor can be read, and issues around seduction, above.) It is therefore difficult to measure the extent of sexual harassment, though it occurs frequently. (To give references to support this point would seem like having to provide bibliographical support for the statement that water runs downhill!) But there is of course a Catch 22. If women ignore such treatment, it proves it is not there; and if they object, try to substantiate that it is occuring, and demand action against it, they are selfish and vindictive in threatening good men's careers (with an added edge if they are black women and the man in question is also black). Few women who fight academic discrimination achieve victory, and, as Caplan says, it is demoralizing to find that although the fight has a strong negative impact on the protesters, regardless of whether they win or lose, the institution itself changes little.

Women find the best source of help with this and other sources of stress is other women. While men with stress turn to their spouse or parents (Barnett in Vartuli 1982: 66), all the writers in the field emphasize the importance of female networks in providing not only support but also solutions – and fun – up to and beyond doctoral level study. But again, of course, the possibility of establishing such networks depends on the physical presence of women in the institution. It is difficult to establish women's groups if most women students are part-time, or if there are not many postgraduates in your field (e.g. in social work or architecture, see Figure 9.2). Moses advocates group research to maintain confidence and connectedness,

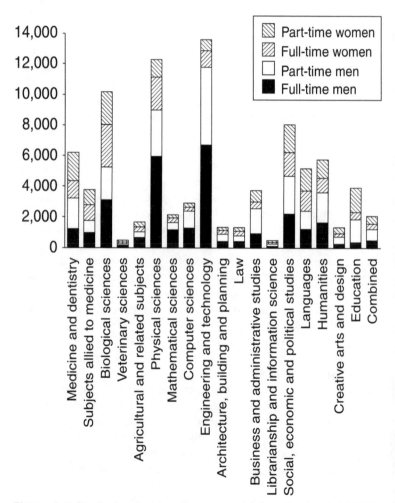

Figure 9.2 Students studying for research degrees in the UK in 1994–5, by sex and subject of study
Source: HESA 1996, Tables 1c and 1g

while Salmon (1992) suggests using mutually supportive group meetings facilitated by the supervisor, rather than (or in addition to) one-to-one supervision.

It is helpful to have formalized seminar programmes for peer stimulation and support and it is especially helpful to women if these contain a criticial mass of women so that women's concerns are 'normalized' (Schwartz and Lever 1973; Solmon 1976). Being given special attention and being put on a pedestal is almost as difficult to cope with as being patronized, disparaged or ignored. However, black women research students will almost never find themselves in such a 'normalized' situation in the UK (unlike the situation in the black colleges in the US which have helped produce the black élite), and they are very likely to encounter the form of academic racism which consists of whites appearing 'surprised if a Black person runs a meeting efficiently or speaks well publicly. . . . "Expectations are so low that when you outstrip their expectation, they turn around and become almost a fan"' (Farish, McPake, Powney and Weiner 1995: 9). High visibility, being asked to speak on behalf of your group, to be the token on all the committees, or lecturers introducing a mention of gender or homosexuals when they catch your eye in a seminar, are all ways of never allowing you to forget your sex and sexuality (or age, race, etc.) – and of stressing that what people see when they see you is, above all, your sex, race, age and/or sexuality.

In the seminars and conferences which graduate students attend and in which they must make their mark as part of their academic apprenticeship, individual women find (and all studies on mixed group dynamics confirm) that:

> in a mixed seminar women will talk less than men, will have less impact on the course of the discussion, will be taken less seriously, will have their brilliant insights attributed to men, and will receive fewer detailed comments on their observations.
>
> (Purkiss 1994: 194)

> male academics may listen to women but many do not hear or take up what women say. Men dominate speech interactions by monopolising turn-taking, by speaking longer and thereby maintaining the floor, and by turning up the vocal volume in order to assert dominance and minimise the potential for interruptions.
>
> (Luke 1994: 218)

Moreover, the academic style required in seminars, as in academic papers, is what Purkiss calls a 'rhetoric of dogmatic certainty' which is difficult for the diffident, and which strikes many women as dishonest.

> The lecture and seminar discourse in the social and natural sciences and humanities, remains the terrain of patriarchal knowledge and modes of expression. . . . Intellectual sparring and competitive one-up-'man'ship – the expressive mode of choice among men – is not women's discursive style and is not how most women go about the getting of knowledge . . . even when women have cracked the discursive codes of masculinist intellectual discourse and bureaucratic protocol, many . . . continue to downplay their discursive facility. The reason: verbally assertive women are quickly labelled with pejorative terms which mark these women as 'bitchy' and 'quarrelsome', 'ambitious' and 'aggressive' – the latter qualities valued in men but considered 'unseemly' in women.
>
> (Luke 1994: 216)

Carmen Luke suggests that in such situations women's silence should be recognized as resistance: a refusal to expose the self. Women know that (supposedly) rational argument, not the narratives of experience with which they may be more comfortable or references to the literature they find revelatory, are what count as authoritative discourse in public speech. 'Reference to the scientific and literary canon of male authorship counts as cultural capital, not reference to feminist and/or post-colonial writers' (Luke 1994: 213). Caplan suggests using instead body language and quietly but confidently taking up space when someone is putting you down; continuing talking while looking directly at a person and/or saying 'I haven't finished' if interrupted; or simply refusing to take notes at, or to clear up after, (mixed sex) meetings, as being as effective at upsetting patterns of domination as direct confrontation.

In so far as the rest of life gets mentioned in research on doing a PhD, it has been to focus on the effects of childcare on rates of completion, and the effects of getting a doctorate on employment prospects. For example, Rudd in his *New Look at Postgraduate Failure* says:

> In general what interfers with postgraduate study is not marriage but a family. It is here and only here, that there is a sharp divide between the experience of men and the women I interviewed.

Many of the special difficulties the women meet are clear and obvious.

(Rudd 1985: 52)

He goes on to give examples (pp. 52–5) of women interviewees being called away to pick up a sick child from school, suffering from nausea and medical problems in pregnancy, becoming absorbed in a new baby, and of the demands of caring for pre-school infants. He stresses that mothers have no frequent long stretches of free time and less time overall to study or for the life of the university. He also remarks on husbands moving job and women students having to cope with the removal and a new university. He says there are especial problems for those who start a PhD part-time when they already have a job and/or family: the children get neglected and the spouse gets neglected. At the end, however, he suggests that things can also work the other way round, and that children may be used as a way of getting out of doing a thesis which is not going well – just as child-free women, and men generally, may use getting a job as their excuse.

Rudd applies the same sorts of arguments about causal relationships to the interaction of the PhD and marital life. He found at least twice as many of his respondents got divorced as might be expected, and that the disparity was highest among women (Rudd 1985: 51). He comments that this could be because of the strains doctoral work puts on marriage – he cites low income and women not doing the chores – even though he says many spouses are supportive. But he also suggests that it could be, conversely, that divorce puts strains on postgraduate study – loss of finance, emotional distraction, time lost. Or again, that it could be that the same skills are needed to maintain marriage as to complete a PhD – so those who fail one, fail the other. In his comments on marriage, however, unlike his comments on childcare, Rudd talks of 'spouses' and does not differentiate wives and husbands, whereas one of Phil Salmon's informants, who got her PhD and a divorce, gives a different twist:

There were those who delighted in [my] development and in my growing courage to express who I was, rather than merely to facilitate others. Others did not find it so easy, including my husband. On the surface, he actively supported my progress. But, sensing his gradual withdrawal, I would often express my concern that he was holding back things that could only damage us in the long term. I used to plead with him to be open, and not to let us go under for the sake of 'just a PhD'. He continued to assert that no, everything was fine. He continued to take the greater share of household tasks. But as he said to a friend, several months after we split up, he realised how much responsibility I had taken previously for the 'real work' of our relationship. During those last two years of the PhD, I was suddenly not there in the same way. And instead of allowing us space to work through what we were both experiencing in terms of our relationship, and to make informed choices about our future if that were necessary, he chose to find another woman on whom to lean. Who was just starting on her career.

(Salmon 1992: 61–2)

If one reverses the sexes in this account, it is less credible, which makes clear the different 'labour relations' of men and women in marriage – on which I have written exhaustively elsewhere (see Delphy and Leonard 1992). Liberal husbands may not contest the division of labour or begrudge the fees, but they may pull the plug if they are not emotionally serviced. Wives are more likely to support their husbands through the uphill struggle to completion.

COMPLETION

Despite the long haul, some men and women do manage to finish their theses and gain their PhD – though many do not complete, especially in the arts and social sciences and especially among part-timers. A study of six UK universities for the Winfield report (Young *et al.* 1987) showed a four-year submission rate in social sciences varying from 30.5 per cent to only 6.6 per cent – but since 1985 procedures have been greatly tightened up and departments now have to achieve a rate of 50 per cent submission within four years to continue to be eligible to supervise ESRC-funded students, so the statistics are changing rapidly. The British Academy's survey of humanities students in 1991 indicated only a third of their award holders were submitting a thesis within four years; half were completing within six years; but approximately a third were not completing at all (British Academy/CVCP 1992 quoted in Burgess, Hogan, Pole, and Sanders 1995: 145).

Women take longer to complete than men – so if success is defined as completing within four years, fewer women are 'successful'.

However, most students want to complete per se, not within four years, and then it is harder to be certain about the relative perform- ance of the sexes. Becher suggests that 'Most academics [a]re under the impression that women are more likely to drop out than men, often for domestic or personal reasons' (Becher 1993: 141), but that:

> Figures for dropouts [i.e. those who embark on a doctorate but withdraw before the end of the four years] [a]re not easy to obtain from ... departments. ... Such information is sensitive, the question is not clear-cut ... [and] some evidence indicates that the women students who do survive [attrition in the initial months and a competitive, strongly male-dominated environment] have a significantly better completion record than their male counterparts.
>
> (Becher 1993: 141)

Moses, too, says 'the literature' reports women drop out in larger numbers (Moses 1990: 37), but she found that most heads of departments interviewed 'could remember only [a] few students who had dropped out, and most were certain that women did not drop out in larger numbers than men'; and that it was actually difficult to get hard data because of poor record-keeping:

> departments were not always aware of the status of their students. With long completion times, part-time enrolments, liberal suspen- sion rules, students could easily get lost. Some universities have considerably tightened up the reporting mechanisms, are enforcing maximum completion times, [and] are regulating suspensions – [but] the impact of this on the dropout rates have to be awaited.
>
> (Moses 1990: 37)

Dunkerley and Weeks, using the national database from the CNAA (i.e. the former UK polytechnic and college sector) found that of those registered in social sciences since 1964 who should have completed by 1990, only 39 per cent had got their degree (a third of these within four years), less than 1 per cent failed, 14 per cent were still registered, but a 'staggering' 46 per cent had withdrawn registration. They note, however, that there was

> Little difference ... between the performance of men and women; in fact, outcomes are remarkably similar. Exactly the same per- centage withdrew (46%). ... The major difference between the two lies in whether they complete on time. Here males have a

better performance with 44 percent compared to the female completion rate on time of 32 percent.

(Dunkerley and Weeks 1994: 158)

CONCLUDING REMARKS

In this chapter I have provided a necessarily quick survey of some of the ways in which men's and women's experiences of doctoral studies differ, drawing on work developed over the last twenty years in the fields of gender and education, women's studies, and feminist theory and methodology. At times I have been able to do no more than indicate that 'a wider literature exists'; but the fact that I felt the need to assert and document the research basis for my statements is itself an indication of the widespread ignorance and scepticism as regards gender differences that exists in the 'mainstream' (or, as some would say, malestream) research on higher education.

In the process it might seem that I have merely been noting women's increased participation within a higher education system which had remained broadly the same. But, of course, universities have changed dramatically in the UK and in Australia over the last ten years, and generally, though to a lesser extent, worldwide. Here I can merely note some changes which are affecting, or which in the future may affect, gender relations and doctoral studies.

We have seen a move from 'élite' to 'mass' higher education, with a huge increase in numbers of students at undergraduate and post-graduate levels. In the absence of adequate extra funding, this has resulted in standardization of courses to through-put students as cheaply as possible and 'regimes of surveillance' to ensure teaching 'quality' is achieved and sustained. Universities (and departments and individual academics) are now in competition with each other, attempting to niche market their 'products' and recruit students, especially certain categories of student – including research students and especially full-cost (often overseas) postgraduate students. The advice given to such students by academics has to be 'read' in this context; it is no longer as disinterested as it used to be. But the new situation does mean feminist research is more acceptable and women students now more welcome, especially if the latter are self-funding (Adkins and Leonard 1992).

Other changes include more legal-rational controls on research which have been introduced through research assessment exercises, where institutional performance is tied to funding; a constant stress that policy or economic relevance should determine what is fundable and worthwhile research; and the research councils' intervention into thesis submission rates and the inclusion of taught components on research degrees, which has been discussed throughout this chapter.

There are signs that although the binary divide between polytechnics and universities has gone, there is not going to be parity between institutions. Rather we shall see, as in places like the US and Japan which have long had mass higher education, a differentiation of institutional types and the development of an extended, competitive hierarchy, with research universities and postgraduate training institutions at the top, and those lower down carrying the bulk of lower-level teaching. Women faculty and women doctoral students are likely to be concentrated in lower-status institutions (see Feldman 1974), and within each institution the existing women staff, and the women research students in their future careers, are likely to find themselves positioned as either primarily teachers or contract researchers (Trotman and Robertson, 1991) – either way probably on short-term contracts and possibly part-time (Aziz 1990). This suggests women need more than ever to be careful about the career choices they make.

Within institutions the move to increase staff-student ratios has been associated with structural reorganization and greater managerial power, more emphasis on marketing and business generation, and (supposedly) rationalized and computerized administrative structures. For individual academics the decade since 1980 has seen a 25 per cent rise in student load, a 37 per cent decline in pay and 22 per cent less spent on libraries (Wilson 1991 quoted in Jary and Parker, 1994), with worsening working conditions: more often in dilapidated modern offices rather than quadrangles, with teaching in the evening and during the summer, etc. Their professional self-identity has made them minimize the passing on of these effects to their students, but many have necessarily become more instrumental and rational, looking to build a career and giving the hierarchy at least minimally what it wants, whether that be ritualistic research or working 9–5 in offices or becoming a leader manager or raising more consultancy income. This, plus pressure to publish for personal, departmental and institutional gain, has made staff move away from personalized relationships with students; and conversely has led to the increased use of postgraduates and tutorial assistants as casual (often minimally supervised) workers. Again, women students may find themselves locked into doing too much teaching and giving too much pastoral support to be able to complete their own PhDs.

Another change associated with the 'massification' of higher education is the breaking of the universities' monopoly on knowledge production and dissemination. The graduates and postgraduates universities are now producing in increasing numbers are mainly going to be employed in the expanding knowledge industries *outside* academia – in government research establishments, corporate labs, NGOs, think-tanks and private research institutes. Here new modes of transdisciplinary knowledge are being produced by 'more transient and heterogeneous sets of practitioners, collaborating on a problem defined in a specific and localised context' (Gibbons *et al.* 1994: 3; Clark 1993: 367). This is already very obvious in science, but it is also occurring in the social sciences and humanities, where literary and historical research and development, for instance, is arguably done as much in museums and record offices, for newspapers, magazines, broadcast media and film, associated with cultural tourism and the general heritage industries, advertising, consultancies and quangos, as in universities. Doctoral training may have to become more relevant ('transferable') to this wider range of occupational careers and workplaces, which contains work teams from various disciplines.

A doctorate is, however, not yet required by most employers in the humanities and social sciences areas – indeed it may be seen as an overqualification and too narrow (cf. economics, business and accountancy) – but with credentialization this may change; and it is important that these changes, and their gender dimensions, are monitored. Indeed, feminist research could be seen as one field forging just such changes and stretching the boundaries of what constitutes research, with its stress on transdisciplinarity, relevance to an external constituency, and a special relationship between those studied, researchers and the readers of their books (Reinharz 1992).

A final observation concerns the new internationalization of research training, whereby there is increased mobility for the whole or part of doctoral or post-doctoral training *between* high income countries (e.g. movement within the EU, see Neave 1992). This may become associated – though this is more contentious – with harmonization of admission criteria and standardization of first year courses. The fact that 38 per cent of students from elsewhere in the EU currently studying for their research degrees in the UK are women went unremarked in Figure 9.1; but it will be important to ensure that such exchanges are set up in such a way as to facilitate women's (and other 'minority groups') participation, and (again) that their progress is monitored and encouraged.

NOTES

1 I should like to thank Christina dos Reis Mendes for help in the preparation of this chapter.

REFERENCES

Acker, S. (1992) 'New Perspectives on an Old Problem: the position of women in British higher education', *Higher Education*, 24: 57–75.

Acker, S. (1994) *Gendered Education: Some Reflections on Women, Teaching and Feminism*, Buckingham: Open University Press.

Adkins, L. and Leonard, D. (1992) 'From Academia to the Education Marketplace: United Kingdom Women's Studies in the 1990s', *Women's Studies Quarterly*, XX (Fall/Winter, Special Issue on Women's Studies in Europe): 28–37.

Allen, F. (1994) 'Academic Women in Australia: progress real or imagined?' in S. Stiver Lie, L. Malik and D. Harris (eds) *The Gender Gap in Higher Education*, London: Kogan Page.

Allen, S. and Leonard, D. (1996) 'From Sexual Divisions to Sexualities: changing sociological agendas' in J. Weeks and J. Holland (eds) *Sexual Cultures: Communities, Values and Intimacy*, London: Macmillan.

Astin, H. S. (1969) *The Woman Doctorate in America*, New York: Russell Sage Foundation.

Astin, H. S. and Malik, L. (1994) 'Academic Women in the United States: problems and prospects' in S. Stiver Lie, L. Malik and D. Harris (eds) *The Gender Gap in Higher Education*, London: Kogan Page.

Aziz, A. (1990) 'Women in U.K. Universities. The road to cazualization?' in S. S. Lie and Y. O'Leary (eds) *Storming the Tower: Women in the Academic World*, London: Kogan Page.

Bacchi, C. (1992) 'Sex on Campus – where does "consent" end and harassment begin?', *Australian Universities' Review*, 35(1): 31–6.

Bacchi, C. (1994) '"Consent" or "Coercion"? Removing conflict of interest from staff–student relations', *Australian Universities' Review*, 37 (2): 55–61.

Becher, T. (1993) 'Graduate Education in Britain: the view from the ground' in B. Clark (ed) *The Research Foundations of Graduate Education: Germany, Britain, France, United States, Japan*, Berkeley: University of California Press.

Blackstone, T. (1975) 'Women Academics in Britain' in D. Warren Piper (ed.) *Women in Higher Education*, London: University of London Teaching Methods Unit.

British Academy/CVCP (1992) *Postgraduate Research in the Humanities: Final Report*, London: British Academy.

Burgess, R. G. (ed.) (1994) *Postgraduate Education and Training in Social Sciences: Processes and Products*, London: Jessica Kingsley.

Burgess, R. G., Hogan, J. V., Pole, C. J. and Sanders, L. (1995) 'Postgraduate Research Training in the United Kingdom' in OECD (ed.) *Research Training: Present and Future*, Paris: OECD.

Cahn, S. M. (ed.) (1990) *Morality, Responsibility, and the University: Studies in Academic Ethics*, Philadelphia: Temple University Press.

Caplan, P. J. (1994) *Lifting a Ton of Feathers: A Woman's Guide to Surviving in the Academic World*, Toronto: University of Toronto Press.

Carter, P. and Jeffs, T. (1992) 'The Hidden Curriculum: sexuality in professional education' in P. Carter, T. Jeffs and M. K. Smith (eds) *Changing Social Work and Welfare*, Buckingham: Open University Press.

Centra, J. A. (1974) *Women, Men and the Doctorate*, Princeton: Educational Testing Service.

Channell, J. (1990) 'The Student–Tutor Relationship' in M. Kinnell (ed.) *The Learning Experiences of Overseas Students*, Buckingham and Bristol: SRHE and Open University Press.

Clark, B. (ed.) (1993) *The Research Foundations of Graduate Education: Germany, Britain, France, United States, Japan*, Berkeley: University of California Press.

Conrad, L. (1994) 'Gender and Postgraduate Supervision' in O. Zuber-Skerritt and Y. Ryan (eds) *Quality in Postgraduate Education*, London: Kogan Page.

Delamont, S. (1989) 'Gender and British Postgraduate Funding Policy: a critique of the Winfield Report', *Gender and Education*, 1(1): 51–7.

Delphy, C. and Leonard, D. (1992) *Familiar Exploitation: A New Analysis of Marriage in Contemporary Western Societies*, Cambridge: Polity Press.

Dunkerley, D. and Weeks, J. (1994) 'Social Science Research Degrees: completion times and rates' in R. Burgess (ed.) *Postgraduate Education and Training in the Social Sciences*, London: Jessica Kingsley.

Farish, M., McPake, J., Powney, J. and Weiner, G. (1995) *Equal Opportunities in Colleges and Universities: Towards Better Practices*, Buckingham: SRHE and Open University Press.

Feldman, S. (1974) *Escape from the Doll's House*, New York: McGraw Hill.

Filteau, C. (ed.) (1989) *Proceedings of a Conference on Women in Graduate Studies in Ontario*, Toronto: Ontario Council on Graduate Studies.

Gallop, J. (1993) 'Consenting Adults', *24 Hours* (November): 49–52.

Gibbons, M., Limoges, C., Nowotny, H., Schwartzman, S., Scott, P. and Trow, M. (1994) *The New Production of Knowledge: The Dynamics of Science and Research in Contemporary Societies*, London: Sage.

Glaser, R. D. and Thorpe, J. S. (1986) 'Unethical Intimacy: a survey of sexual contact and advances between psychology educators and female graduate students', *American Psychologist*, 41(1): 43–51.

Gold, A. (1995) 'Working with Silences' in K. Hämäläinen, D. Oldroyd and E. Haapanen (eds) *Making School Improvement Happen*, Vantaa: University of Helsinki.

Goldsmith, J. and Shawcross, V. (1985) *It Ain't Half Sexist, Mum: Women as Overseas Students in the United Kingdom*, London: World University Service.

HESA (1996) *Students in Higher Education Institutions 1994–95*, Bristol: HESA.

Hockey, J. (1991) 'The Social Science PhD: a literature review', *Studies in Higher Education*, 16(3): 319–32.

Holmstrom, E. I. and Holmstrom, R. W. (1974) 'Plight of the Woman Doctoral Student', *American Educational Research Journal*, 11 (Winter): 1–17.

Jary, D. and Parker, M. (1994) 'The Neo-Fordist University: academic work and mass higher education (or any colour you like as long as its . . .)', paper presented to 1994 BSA Conference.

Katz, J. and Hartnett, R. T. (eds) (1976) *Scholars in the Making*, Cambridge, Mass.: Ballinger Publishing Co.

Lewins, H. (1990) 'Living Needs' in M. Kinnell (ed.) *The Learning Experiences of Overseas Students*, Buckingham and Bristol: SRHE and Open University Press.

Lewis, M. G. (1993) *Without a Word: Teaching Beyond Women's Silence*, New York: Routledge.

Luke, C. (1994) 'Women in the Academe: the politics of speech and silence', *British Journal of Sociology of Education*, 15(2): 211–30.

Mintz, G. (pseudonym) (1967) 'Some Observations on the Function of Women Sociologists at Sociology Conferences', *The American Sociologist* (August): 158–9.

Moses, I. (1990) *Barriers to Women's Participation as Postgraduate Students*, Canberra: Australian Government Publishing Service.

Moses, I. (1992) 'Quality in PhD Education – issues in women's participation' in D. J. Cullen (ed.) *Quality in PhD Education*, Canberra: CEDAM and the Graduate School, ANU.

Moses, I. (1994) 'Planning for Quality in Graduate Studies' in O. Zuber-Skerrit and Y. Ryan (eds) *Quality in Postgraduate Education*, London: Kogan Page.

Neave, G. (1992) 'On the Casting of Bread upon the Waters: higher education and Western European integration', *Compare*, 22(1): 5–15.

Orlans, K. P. M. (ed.) (1994) *Gender and the Academic Experience*, Lincoln and London: University of Nebraska Press.

Pahl, J. (1989) *Money and Marriage*, London: Macmillan.

Phillips, E. M. and Pugh, D. (1994) *How to Get a PhD: A Handbook for Students and their Supervisors*, 2nd edn, Buckingham: Open University Press.

Powles, M. (1986) 'Chips in the Wall? Women and postgraduate study', *Australian Universities Review*, 29: 33–7.

Purkiss, D. (1994) 'The Lecherous Professor Revisited: Plato, pedagogy and the scene of harassment' in C. Brant and Y. Lee Too (eds) *Rethinking Sexual Harassment*, London: Pluto Press.

Ramazanoglu, C. (1987) 'Sex and Violence in Academic Life or You Can Keep a Good Woman Down' in J. Hanmer and M. Maynard (eds) *Women, Violence and Social Control*, London: Macmillan.

Reinharz, S. (1992) *Feminist Methods in Social Research*, New York: Oxford University Press.

Rendel, M. (1975) 'Men and Women in Higher Education', *Educational Review*, 27: 192–210.

Roiphe, K. (1993) *The Morning After: Sex, Fear and Feminism*, London: Hamish Hamilton.

Rudd, E. (1985) *A New Look at Postgraduate Failure*, Guildford: SRHE and NFER-Nelson.

Rudd, E. in association with Simpson, R. (1975) *The Highest Education: A Study of Graduate Education in Britain*, London: Routledge and Kegan Paul.

Salmon, P. (1992) *Achieving a PhD – Ten Students' Experience*, Stoke-on-Trent: Trentham Books.

Sandler, B. and Hall, R. M. (1986) *The Campus Climate Revisited: Chilly for Women Faculty, Administrators and Graduate Students*, Washington: Association of American Colleges.

Schwartz, P. and Lever, J. (1973) 'Women in the Male World of Higher Education' in A. Rossi and A. Calderwood (eds) *Academic Women on the Move*, New York: Russell-Sage Foundation.

Scott, S. and Porter, M. (1983) 'On the Bottom Rung: a discussion of women's work in sociology', *Women's Studies International Forum*, 6(2): 211–21.

Skeggs, B. (1995) 'Women's Studies in Britain in the 1990s: entitlement cultures and institutional contraints', *Women's Studies International Forum*, 18(4): 475–85.

Smith, D. (1978) 'A Peculiar Eclipsing: women's exclusion from men's culture', *Women's Studies International Forum*, 1, 281–95.

Solmon, L. C. (1976) *Male and Female Graduate Students: The Question of Equal Opportunity*, New York: Praeger.

Taylorson, D. (1980) 'Highly educated women: a sociological study of women PhD candidates', PhD dissertation, University of Manchester.

Taylorson, D. (1984) 'The Professional Socialization, Integration and Identity of Women PhD Candidates' in S. Acker and D. Warren Piper (eds) *Is Higher Education Fair to Women?*, Guildford: SRHE and NFER-Nelson.

Thomas, K. (1990) *Gender and Subject in Higher Education*, Buckingham: Open University Press.

Trotman, J. and Robertson, S. (1991) 'Taking the Queen's Shilling: public policy research and academics in the 1990s' mimeo, Institute for Public Policy Research, Edith Cowan University, Western Australia.

Unterhalter, E. and Maxey, K. (1995) *Educating South Africans in Britain and Ireland: A Review of Thirty Years of Sponsorship by the Africa Educational Trust*, London: RESA, Institute of Education, University of London.

Vartuli, S. (ed.) (1982) *The PhD Experience*, New York: Praeger.

Williams, G., Blackstone, T. and Metcalfe, D. (1974) *The Academic Labour Market: Economic and Social Aspects of a Profession*, London: Elsevier.

Williams, R. (1982) 'In and Out of Relationships: a serious game for the woman doctoral student' in S. Vartuli (ed.) *The PhD Experience*, New York: Praeger.

Wilson, T. (1991) 'The Proletarianisation of Academic Labour', *Industrial Relations Journal*, 22(4): 250–62.

Winfield, G. (1987) *The Social Science PhD: The ESRC Enquiry on Submission Rates*, London: Economic and Social Research Council.

Woodhall, M. (1975) 'The Economic Benefits of Education for Women' in D. Warren Piper (ed.) *Women in Higher Education*, London: University of London Teaching Methods Unit.

Young, K., Fogarty, M. and McRae, S. (1987) *The Management of Doctoral Studies in the Social Sciences*, London: Policy Studies Institute.

Chapter 10

Comparative perspectives on the British PhD

Robert Cowen

A thesis for the PhD degree must form a distinct contribution to the knowledge of the subject and afford evidence of originality shown by the discovery of new facts and/or by the exercise of independent critical power.

(University of London, *Regulations for Internal Students*, 1994–5: 1509)

INTRODUCTION

'Getting' a PhD is a lonely business, interrupted only by informal chats with an indifferent supervisor. The PhD is written by the research candidate in a social vacuum and is mainly of interest to proud parents. The PhD leads nowhere, occupationally, and the process of gaining a PhD is best described as a scholarly chore which involves demonstrating great learning about a little topic. The argument of this chapter is that these propositions are small truths in the British context currently: advanced academic studies have changed dramatically in the last decade in ways which have redefined the nature of the PhD and doctoral work. However, what is increasingly true is that gaining a PhD is more and more a test of self-organization, of institutional organization, and less and less a test of original critical intellectual power.

How we have come to this – the bureaucratization of originality – is an interesting story, which is partly the history of an imaginative and visionary ideal being moved between countries and being redefined and used in different ways in different social contexts. It is also the story of the corruption of an ideal, in its country of origin, and the use of the ideal for other purposes in other places. Right now, the older ideal of the doctorate is again changing in Britain under the impact of contemporary ideologies of management. But the story of these multiple changes begins in nineteenth-century Germany.

A MOVING IDEA

Much of the 'myth' of a PhD, as a lonely business of making a major contribution to knowledge and creating a *magnum opus* under a solitary supervisor, has its roots in the social origins of what became a world model. The model was originally German, inspired by the ideas and reforms of Wilhelm von Humboldt, and gives us such internationally understood concepts as 'seminar', such internationally misunderstood concepts as 'the' doctorate, and the peculiar practices and esoteric techniques of the *Doktorvater*; a term for 'supervisor' which fortunately did not gain international currency. The model also gives us an initial definition of the socially marginal condition of the doctoral candidate, hoping for a career, thinking original thoughts, but living in a structured situation of professional dependence.

In the vision of von Humboldt, the university would be a very special institution, engaged in a continuous and organized search for absolute truth. All academic learning and research would be defined by this goal. The vision was an educational one – people would be changed, in ways central to their identity, by the experience:

> Everything depends upon holding to the principle of considering knowledge . . . as something not yet found, never completely to be discovered, and searching relentlessly for it as such. As soon as one ceases actually to seek knowledge or imagines that it does not have to be pulled from the depths of the intellect, but rather can be arranged in some exhaustive array through meticulous collection, then everything is irretrievably and forever lost. . . . This is because knowledge alone, which comes from and can be planted in the depths of spirit, also transforms character; and for the state, just as for humanity, facts and discourse matter less than character and behaviour.
>
> (Fallon 1980: 25 Humboldt quoted in)

This vision represented a break from the German (and European) eighteenth-century concern for the preparation, in academies and vocational schools, of an administrative élite. Now, that is from about the first decade of the nineteenth century with the founding of the University of Berlin, the university had its own mission, and was to be separated from society through the clarity of its own purposes, serving society in its own way and on its own terms (Gellert 1993: 4).

Inside the university both teacher and student would pursue 'truth as such'. The teacher, more experienced and with more work already accomplished, would guide the student, but both teacher and student would do research. Teaching would primarily be an account of on-going research, usually the professor's research or the research of those who were working with him (sic) in his institute or his seminar. There would be a unity of research and teaching (*die Einheit von Forschung und Lehre*) with the emphasis on the import-ance of scholarship, confirming and extending 'the value of scholarly methods of inquiry at the frontiers of knowledge. Humboldt acknow-ledged this principle by appointing the best scholars available, encouraging them to continue their research, and making them collectively responsible for academic standards and the award of degrees' (Fallon 1980: 28).

This vision created four principles and four sets of practices, which had some long-term effects. The freedom of the student to learn underpinned the geographic mobility of German students in the nineteenth century – they could pursue their research where they saw fit, learning from a range of teachers in different universities. The professor was excused from having to develop a concern for ped-agogic process; lecturing was merely a set of reflections by a scholar on research-in-progress, and routine lectures were normally limited to two a week anyway. The main arena for work for the teacher and the student was a research-oriented seminar or an institute, admis-sion to which was controlled by the professor. And the professor had freedom of research in his own knowledge domain.

In practice, of course, the model was affected by the division of both academic and professional labour in German society of that period. The Humboldt reforms redressed the balance of power within the university, downgrading the privileges and dominance of the old professional faculties of theology, law and medicine, for which the arts and sciences faculties had merely been preparatory. 'In fact, the philosophical faculty became the most important' (Ben-David 1977: 20–1).

In practice also, Humboldt's reforms linked the schools and the university and the state, because certification of *Gymnasium* teachers was mandatory through a comprehensive state examination, the preparation for which was done in the university. In Berlin, the only degree was the doctorate, though most students did not complete this, aiming instead at the *Staatsexamen*, the qualifying examinations for entry into the civil service or teaching in a *Gymnasium* (Fallon 1980: 17–18). Where students did, however, wish to complete a formal academic degree, they followed a similar curriculum to that of the *Staatsexamen*, but were required to obtain access to a professor who agreed to supervise the work and 'in the authoritarian climate of nineteenth century Germany, this doctoral supervisor was formally called the student's Doktorvater' (Fallon 1980: 40).

In practice also, this vision of *Bildung durch Wissenschaft* (education through science/the search for truth) took on a particular social form. The professors of Germany gained great power inside the university, the university itself fractured into specialist groups, the power of sponsorship of professors increased dramatically as examinations, especially the *Habilitation*, were introduced to select potential future professors who taught as unpaid lecturers while waiting for a chair. All of this not only placed the professor at the centre of the university affairs (as compared, for example, with state officials, university administrators, or students), but also reproduced and magnified, inside the university, some of the inequalities of the wider society. Finally, by the end of the nineteenth century, the university was also drawn into German efforts to industrialize the economy and to strengthen the nation's power position internationally. Well before the traumas of the Weimar regime, the Humboldtian vision began to be lost, at home.

Nevertheless, a pattern had been set. *Lernfreiheit* – the freedom of the student to learn and indeed to wander – had set a pattern of the loneliness of research, a pattern which continues in Germany in particular today, where many doctoral candidates work primarily at home. *Lehrerfreiheit*, the freedom of the teacher to pursue his or her research, was later confirmed in what was then West Germany in the *Grundgesetz*, the Constitutional Law. *Lehrerfreiheit* permitted high levels of specialization, an impolite and pejorative phrase for which is: 'Knowing more and more about less and less.' The idea of the *Doktorvater*, and working within a specialist seminar or an institute with career prospects dependent on the sponsorship of a senior academic, defined the dependency relations of the doctoral candidate. Even teaching as part of the duties of the professorial candidate-in-waiting (in Germany, *the Privatdozent* already possessing the *Habilitation* and a degree) is an idea which reappears strongly in the graduate schools of the United States in recent times.

However unattractive this model may seem to contemporary generations of doctoral candidates, it represented, for earnest young scholars of many nations in the late nineteenth century, a unique opportunity. Up until the 1870s the German university was the only one, at that time in the world, which had geared itself around the idea of research, and it was the only place where a sustained research training could be acquired (Ben-David 1977: 22). The number of British students at German universities rose from twenty-six in 1835–6 to 137 in 1891–2, and in that year the number of Americans in German universities was 446 (Simpson 1983: 17). The attraction was particularly noticeable in certain disciplinary areas, such as chemistry and later history, but the general reputation and the world dominance of the German university as an academic model was widely recognized overseas; not least in the US and the UK.

In the latter part of the nineteenth century, both the United States and the UK were defining their university systems by pulling together a plethora of higher education institutions, and both countries were on the edge of creating a profession of learning. So at different speeds, and with different difficulties, both the US and the UK mixed the reform of their universities and the creation of the academic profession with the importation of the idea of a doctorate.

In the United States, the higher education system had expanded rapidly with a variety of new colleges (including both religious colleges and the so-called Land-Grant Colleges founded after 1862) which existed alongside the older colleges and universities such as William and Mary, Harvard and Yale:

The first Ph.D was awarded in 1861 by Yale. . . . Yet it was not until the 1880s that anything like a modern university really took shape in America. Perhaps the most important breakthroughs were the founding of Johns Hopkins and Clark as primarily graduate universities. Eliot's success in instituting the elective system at Harvard was also important, both in its own right and because it facilitated the assemblage of a more scholarly and specialized faculty. The 1890s saw further progress, with the founding of Chicago, the reform of Columbia, and the tentative acceptance of graduate work as an important activity in the leading state universities. This was also the period when national learned societies and journals were founded and when knowledge was broken up into its present departmental categories ('physics,' 'biology,' 'history,' 'philosophy,' and so forth), with the department emerging as the basic unit of academic administration. Medicine and law also became serious subjects of graduate study at this time, with Johns Hopkins leading the way in medicine and Harvard in law.

(Jencks and Reisman 1968: 13)

The mixture of processes – the consolidation and standardization of the esoteric knowledge of the legal and medical professions, the redefinition of the higher education system, the specification of one of the basic units of American academic life, the department, and the importation of the doctorate with its possibilities for the certification of a profession of learning – are all visible in this period from the 1860s to 1900. However, the doctorate was an extra layer on a system with very varied standards, and it took some time for the bachelor, master's and doctoral degree system to be stabilized. In ways that reverberate with the 1990s, this occurred partly under the pressure of working out international equivalences so that foreign university systems, the English and especially the German, might be able to decide on the acceptability of American applicants with 'good' bachelor degrees. The system was in fact stabilized in the first few years of the twentieth century by the Carnegie Foundation and the new Association of American Universities: a list of universities of good standing was worked out and the results sent to Germany in 1913, and to the UK in 1916 (Simpson 1983: 20). In the United States the award of the PhD, which by the 1920s and 1930s had spread to the big state universities, became an important and, later, a definitive criterion for admission to the profession of learning: the academic profession. For selection into that, a system of qualifications had been established.

In the United Kingdom, the nineteenth century saw the consolidation of the professions and the redefinition of the higher and university system. New universities were created in most of the industrial cities, including London in 1828, and elsewhere medical, technical and commercial colleges were amalgamated to form university colleges and ultimately universities in such cities as Manchester, Liverpool, Leeds, Birmingham, and Sheffield (by 1905). In the new university in London:

The education was consciously geared to the professions. Chairs were established in medicine, jurisprudence, political economy, chemistry, natural philosophy (physics), as well as in modern languages, logic and the philosophy of the human mind, and

planned in engineering (not filled until 1841), mineralogy, design
and education – almost every subject, in fact, except theology. The
medical school proved to be the lynch-pin of the enterprise,
attracting three-quarters of all the students in 1834. James Bryce
. . . began the training of teachers there in 1836.

(Perkin 1969: 17–18)

However, there were also problems. In the nineteenth century the
universities of Oxford and Cambridge had not only been going
through a difficult period which inspired Commissions of Inquiry,
but their college cultures, based very much in the teaching of
undergraduates, made it difficult for them to develop a research
orientation (Simpson 1983: 22–7). Strenuous efforts over a period of
sixty years led to a gradual rebalancing of the national system and
the addition of a research dimension. The anxieties were multiple,
but international economic competition with Germany and the
United States was clarifying some of the weaknesses of the British
higher education system, especially in scientific research. There was
experimentation with the creation of DSc degrees (initially by
examination) in London and increasing pressure in Oxford and
Cambridge, especially from the scientists who had studied in Germany or were impressed by that system, to sort out the possibility of
a research award. Slowly the idea of the award of advanced degrees,
based on thesis work, began to be accepted by University Senates.

But it took a war with Germany for the British system – keen to
divert young Americans to come under British cultural influence by
studying in the UK rather than Germany – to take major steps. The
Foreign Office itself, building on a movement within the universities,
assisted in encouraging the creation of a PhD degree structure.
Oxford established a PhD (technically a D.Litt) in 1917, and was
followed by other universities such as Cambridge, London and
several northern universities (Simpson 1983: 135–59). The pressure
of international political, economic, and cultural competition had
broken through the difficulties and inertia. The PhD had been
established, offering the long-term possibility that it would become
a minimum condition for admission into the academic profession.

Thus, the possibility for a profession of learning, guarded at its
entry by a PhD, was now established in both countries. Between the
countries, there were, of course, differences which affected developments in the next sixty years. For example, the wider variation in
standards in the universities of the United States contrasted with the

relatively homogeneous standards in the UK – until the British government by legislative action almost doubled the number of UK universities in the early 1990s. Although there was a rapid growth in the numbers of PhDs taken in the United Kingdom in the ten years after 1917 (Simpson 1983: 160–5), there was an even faster growth in the rate of doctoral awards in the United States through the big state universities in the 1920s and 1930s. In the 1960s in the UK (and in the US) there was a great increase in the number of taught master's degrees, but the same period in the United States saw the consolidation of the research and development industry, of which the doctorate was part, under the stress of economic, technological and political competition with the Soviet Union. In Britain the continuation of the tradition of the professor as head of department for life (until the mid-1970s) tended to reinforce the German pattern of the *Doktorvater*. This tradition was broken quite rapidly in the United States where departmental structures contained layers of professors (assistant, associate and full) with an elected chairperson running a department for a short period of time.

Despite these differences, there was a major similarity: a qualification system had been formed, marked by governmental preferences 'for entrusting professional education to academic institutions rather than to apprenticeship and courses organized by the professional associations' (Ben-David 1977: 37). The universities of the United States and the United Kingdom had consolidated the training structures for various professions. With the PhD they had also begun the refinement of the socialization and selection system for their own, the profession of learning.

In both the USA and the UK, the doctoral degree had been added to the sequence of bachelor and master's degrees. This piece of cultural borrowing would be costly in terms of time and money for future generations of American and British students; but now paths into the academic profession were clearer in both countries although the speed at which the doctorate affected hiring practices would vary between the two countries.

THE DOCTORATE TODAY

Economic and political motifs, similar to those which had affected the importation of the doctorate into the US and the UK from Germany in the early twentieth century, are taking a reprise in the late twentieth century as many of the OECD countries review the nature of their doctoral provision (OECD 1995). Many countries are now alert to the idea of competition in a world 'knowledge economy' in which wealth is generated by intellectual innovation (as, for example, in bio-technology, or information technology), and in which the concentration of economic power in North America and north-west Europe can no longer be expected to continue on the old terms (Cowen 1996a). Thus both the US and the UK, at the policy level, are taking steps to sort out their national research and development capacities, including the expansion and reform of their doctoral systems.

The consequence is that working for a doctorate remains an individual act, but is also a social and political one. Doctoral research candidates are, with increasing frequency, tightly organized in groups, in time, and in social space inside their institutions. Nationally, doctoral candidates are becoming part of big bureaucracies devoted to advanced training. At national and institutional levels, doctoral programmes are being increasingly codified and routinized, and made subject to quality control checks. The rather detailed specification of sequences in a doctoral programme has been for quite some time typical of the United States – the sketch below is partly drawn from the author's personal experience in a major state university for five years in the early 1970s; and the pattern has begun to affect the social science doctorate in Britain.

The style of the American doctorate, and ways of working for it, have been affected by the elective system of undergraduate credits, in which graduation is achieved by the accumulation of 'credit hours' – fundamentally a system for measuring time (class attendance), writing (of semester-papers) and knowledge domain (courses will be planned to cover 'major' and 'minor' areas of expertise). The initial work for a PhD in the United States is not dissimilar: the accumulation of course credits across an appropriate range of disciplinary fields, which are likely to be useful for work in that thesis area and on that thesis topic. There will be an expectation of the maintenance of reasonable grades in the courses attended, normally expressed in a faculty or graduate school requirement as a certain QPA – a 'quality point average'. Toward the end of this sequence of courses there would also probably be a 'comprehensive examination', individually set but taken by all candidates to demonstrate that they have mastered sufficient of the associated knowledge domains to begin, with full concentration, the writing of the doctoral 'dissertation' (Gumpert 1993; Clark 1993).

The writing of the dissertation by the candidate him- or herself will be guided by a dissertation committee, probably at least three people, perhaps four. The shape and lines of argument of the thesis will be hammered out in this committee, where a great deal of the quality control work on the thesis is done. The candidate must convince the committee that the major methodological and methods choices of the theories are clearly and correctly made and displayed, and that an appropriate range of intellectual perspectives has been brought to bear on the thesis. These processes are likely to be supplemented by a full public presentation of the doctoral dissertation proposal within a seminar open to the faculty (Lapidus *et. al.* 1995; Clark 1993).

Thus the American PhD can and should be seen as a highly structured experience, with a number of checkpoints built into the process. The accumulation of course credits and quality point averages, comprehensive examinations, the appointment of a dissertation committee, a formal, even a public, proposal of a thesis topic, and the allowance of more course credits for the writing of the dissertation itself, add up to a considerable sequence of controls over the timing and pacing of the preparation – over access to the start line. Rather charmingly there is even a phrase 'ABD' which means that a candidate has finished a doctorate – 'all but dissertation'. (In other words, in English terms, the candidate has not begun the main task – writing a thesis.) Less charmingly, each of the quality control points means the possibility of an individual being 'cooled out' of the system in the first couple of years. However, the system also means progression through the system with a peer group, perhaps less loneliness because of class attendance, and often smaller and shorter 'theses' (written in the second couple of years) than would be normal for a British social science doctorate.

In other words, moving toward the American experience of 'working for a doctorate' changes the rules of the game to:

- a large taught element,
- a clear sequence of points of progression through a 'doctoral program',
- the absence of a *Doktorvater* and thus less intense and personalized pedagogic relations,
- and, often, a shorter dissertation, though one in which control of techniques of research will be very clear.

The UK universities are now defining in increasing detail the organization of doctoral study which means that something like a national *system* of doctoral supervision in the social sciences is being created, that under external pressure codification of quality processes is occurring, and that a high degree of surface convergence to the American model is more and more visible.

The reasons are national. The British government has placed the university, its knowledge productivity and its contribution to Britain's economic position at the centre of a long national debate about the purposes and shape of formal education. Since 1979 considerable effort, marked by national legislation, has gone into redefining higher education. This legislation altered the number of universities, to whom they should be responsible, their financial basis, and the rules for measuring their productivity and the ways they, their departments and even – by extension – individual academics would be managed and evaluated (Cowen 1991). The debate has been handled at the national level through the explicit rationale of 'quality', used in phrases such as quality audit, quality control and total quality management (Barnett 1992). The pattern of actual control, however, is fordist: top-down management, careful counting of a supposedly standard product (a book is a book; and an article is an article), detailed routine controls on production processes especially time, and payment where possible by piece-rates. Thus national managerial groups (the Higher Education Funding Councils) apply standard measures of 'quality' to the performance of about ninety universities. National rules define time periods in which productivity (in published research output, in teaching, in the gaining of money for research, in increases in student numbers, and in PhD graduation rates) will be measured. The income of universities is increased or diminished by how these national management criteria indicate a university has performed.

Within this process of constructing greater measurable and measured efficiency the PhD did not escape. The PhD is now construed as important in the national effort to train skilled manpower; as involving not only opportunity costs for individuals but also direct costs to the research-funding agencies and research councils; as unsatisfactory in terms of completion rates, in particular in the social sciences; and as something for which training is necessary. The debate about length of training and the balance of training started a decade ago with the Report of the Advisory Board for the Research Councils, in 1988. The idea of a four-year doctorate was proposed, and problems of poor supervision, poor student motivation and lack of knowledge of research techniques were to be addressed. The

Economic and Social Research Council proposed a 'black-list'. That is, failure to achieve a 50 per cent graduation rate over four years for ESRC-financed students would draw sanctions against the institution. The theme of inserting a taught element, emphasizing research techniques, was stressed by the Committee of Vice-Chancellors and Principals as early as 1988 (Burgess *et. al.* 1995).

The consequences of this decade of debate have included a formalization of the process, following the ESRC model, where institutions have developed systematic training courses in research, clarified and tightened supervisory responsibilities, required annual reports on each student, and often encouraged some form of written memorandum after each tutorial to consolidate advice. Most universities are now experimenting with joint supervision (as a minimum) and have established department level research committees to monitor the progress of all research candidates.

The most recent review of postgraduate education, in May 1996, stresses a code of good practice which should ensure that supervisors are themselves active researchers, that doctoral candidates have 'pre-specified appropriate back up supervisory arrangements, and that there be regular monitoring and assessment of progress' (Harris Report 1996: 45). In an innovative suggestion the report codifies all postgraduate education into levels and, explicitly and deliberately 'using an American-style system of designating levels', sees a PhD as being marked by the accumulation of credits for taught courses, in addition to thesis completion (Harris Report 1996: 96–7).

A central point about all of these pressures is that they are external. They find their sources in the concerns of the national government and are expressed through the specific policies of a number of national agencies involved in the evaluation industry and in the research industry. Under these external pressures, several institutions (Warwick in 1991, University College, London in 1992) have now evolved the functional equivalent of the American 'graduate school' – a special section of the university which takes as its central concern facilities for, and the progress of, research candidates (Burgess *et al.* 1995). Sequences of training have been organized, check points (e.g. literature surveys or methods chapters) may now be scrutinized by specialist research lecturers or deans of research, and examining practices have changed. For example, the thesis supervisor would not now normally play an articulate part in the *viva voce* of the doctoral examination.

The crucial difference from the American model – which contains many of these elements – is the power of penetration of these British rules into the details of pedagogic process. Although at the moment British academics still define the examination process, they have less and less control over the terms on which, and the processes through which, a doctoral thesis will be prepared.

The result is an increasing bureaucratization, within doctoral programmes, of time; of pedagogic sequence; of pedagogic relations, through memoranda; and of knowledge, into training modules. Of course the thesis itself could be subjected to bureaucratic requirements at least at the level of chapter sequence: for example, statement of problem; critical account of existing literature; new information or interpretation (two chapters); implications for the existing literature, for future research and for policy. As far as I am aware this has not yet been suggested at the national level but such a proposition would be philosophically coherent within the present context of the de-professionalization of the British university academic. Both doctoral student and supervisor now work within quite tight rule-systems, process checks and timeframes. Some public, external, definition of the correct shape of the thesis itself would now be logical; and the de-personalization and bureaucratization of the process of 'getting' a doctorate could be taken further, for example by emphasizing even more the ideas of relations of contract (rather than personal professional obligation) between doctoral supervisor and doctoral candidate; of *compulsory* learning sequences for doctoral candidates and of national standardization of process checks and timeframes for completion of thesis.

Interestingly, as the academic profession loses control over the terms of its own teaching, writing and supervisory work – work which is increasingly framed and fragmented by academic managers, the bureaucratization of time and process, and the pressures of performativity (Cowen 1996b) – the research 'profession' grows. What we are now seeing, apart from money and 'tax dollar' efficiency, is the creation of a research profession, more specifically a pool of more or less trained researchers with unstable employment prospects who are available for a wide range of short-term research contracts (Henkel and Kogan 1993; Burgess *et al.* 1995). It is of importance that the training of these persons be standardized: that there be a 'professional' training component in individuals' histories and that this package will cover a fairly standard range of topics such as the philosophies of the social sciences, major methodological positions, the ethical and political dimensions of social science research and, above all, that the researchers are skilled in a standard-ized range of techniques – social survey work, interview techniques, statistical packages and so on (Burgess *et al.* 1995). Doctoral candidates are becoming part of a new and crucial quasi-profession of skilled and certified researchers.

As the training of this group becomes standardized, the con-temporary problem of research candidates is that they are not lonely enough – that is, they have less and less time to themselves for reflection, for re-writing and for 'being original'. The PhD is more and more a matter of completing organized sequences of tasks, more and more a matter of providing new information and demonstrating control of research techniques. What we are seeing is the routiniz-ation of the 'production of producers' of knowledge, in Larson's phrase (Larson 1977: 45) and the production of new knowledge through the application of sets of rules.

CONCLUSION

This does not mean that being original, in the sense of being creative and saying something intellectually powerful and theoretically new on the basis of major scholarship, is impossible for doctoral candid-ates in the social sciences. It is merely harder than it used to be. 'Originality' – the originality that gets you a PhD within university regulations – has been routinized: it has become a more or less predictable product of the structural attributes of doctoral pro-grammes such as institutional sequences of training, and the cumu-lative effect of 'quality' control mechanisms.

However, Humboldt's argument quoted earlier that 'As soon as one ceases actually to seek knowledge or imagines that it does not have to be pulled from the depths of the intellect, but rather can be arranged in some exhaustive array through meticulous collection, then everything is irretrievably and forever lost' is incorrect. The search for the demonstration of brilliance and the kind of creative power in scholarship and research which alters fields of study and which universities still seek in their new recruits merely moves elsewhere – to the post-doctoral or to the assistant professor phase of a career, as in the United States, and is judged by publication rather than the PhD.

The existing fordist controls of 'quality' in British universities are national policies. Such policies and practices will probably produce reactions – such as the displacement of British academic talent to the international arena, and reviews of career choices by individuals. The long-term danger is simply that the academic profession, the profession of learning, in Britain will be the long-term loser, if it routinizes social science creativity or even if it 'displaces' it into the equivalent of assistant professorships or post-doctoral fellowships without American-level resources. The long-term danger for UK universities is that the British social science doctorate will become indistinguishable from the American – and the Americans invented the routine-process model, have used it longer, and probably do it better. In a competition for international influence British universities will lose – if the vocabulary can be forgiven – their social science market niche.

Meanwhile the short-term problem for the individual doctoral candidate is that the PhD becomes just one more step in a longer and longer selection process for admission to the academic profession. The paradox is that the price of admission to the British academic profession within a couple of decades is likely to be a book, rather than a PhD; and PhD programmes currently are even worse as a socialization into book writing than the traditional social science thesis. But the good news is that short books (a book is a book) are encouraged now by the crudest national system of quality control among the universities in the western world.

REFERENCES

Barnett, R. (1992) *Improving Higher Education: Total Quality Care*, Buckingham: SRHE and Open University Press.

Ben-David. J. (1977) *Centers of Learning: Britain, France, Germany, United States*, New York: McGraw Hill Book Company.

Burgess, R.G., Hogan, J.V., Pole, C.J. and Sanders, L. (1995) 'Postgraduate research training in the United Kingdom' in OECD *Research Training: Present and Future*, Paris: OECD, 135–58.

Clark, B. (ed.) (1993) *The Research Foundations of Graduation Education: Germany, Britain, France, United States, Japan*, Berkeley: University of California Press.

Cowen, R. (1991) 'The management and evaluation of the entrepreneurial university: the case of England', *Higher Education Policy* 4, 30: 9–13.

Cowen, R. (ed.) (1996a) *The Evaluation of Higher Education Systems: World Yearbook of Education 1996*, London: Kogan Page.

Cowen, R. (1996b) 'Performativity, Post-modernity and the university', *Comparative Education*, 32, 2: 245–58.

Fallon, D. (1980) *The German University: A Heroic Ideal in Conflict with the Modern World*, Boulder: Colorado Associated University Press.

Gellert, C. (1993) 'The German model of research and advanced education' in B. Clark (ed.) *The Research Foundations of Graduate Education: Germany, Britain, France, United States, Japan*, Berkeley: University of California Press.

Gumpert, P. (1993) 'Graduate education and research imperatives: views from American campuses' in B. Clark (ed.) *The Research Foundations of Graduate Education: Germany, Britain, France, United States, Japan*, Berkeley: University of California Press.

Harris Report (1996) *Review of Postgraduate Education*, Bristol: HEFCE, CVCP, SCOP.

Henkel, M. and Kogan, M. (1993) 'Research training and graduate education: the British macro-structure' in B. Clark (ed.) *The Research Foundations of Graduate Education: Germany, Britain, France, United States, Japan*, Berkeley: University of California Press.

Jencks, C. and Reisman, D. (1968) *The Academic Revolution*, New York: Doubleday.

Lapidus, J.B., Syverson, P.D. and Welch, S.R. (1995) 'Postgraduate research training in the United States' in OECD, *Research Training: Present and Future*, Paris: OECD.

Larson, M.S. (1977) *The Rise of Professionalism: A Sociological Analysis*, Berkeley: University of California Press.

OECD (1995) *Research Training: Present and Future*, Paris: OECD.

Perkin, H. (1969) *Key Profession: The History of the Association of University Teachers*, London: Routledge and Kegan Paul.

Simpson, R. (1983) *How the PhD came to Britain: A Century of Struggle for Postgraduate Education*, Guildford: SRHE.

University of London (1994–5) *Regulations for Internal Students*, London: University of London Senate House.

Index